Y0-BCV-897

ANATOMY OF A CHURCH

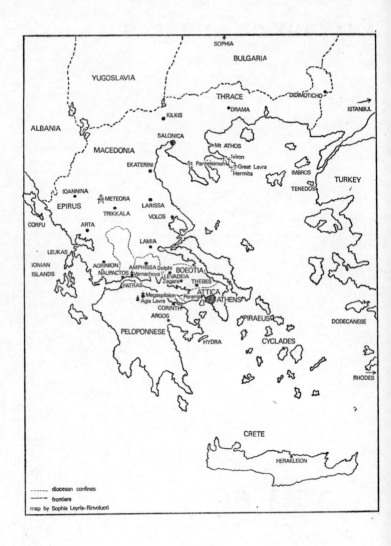

map by Sophie Leyris-Rinvolucri

- - - - - diocesan confines
- - - - frontiers

anatomy of a church

GREEK ORTHODOXY TODAY

by MARIO RINVOLUCRI

With a Foreword by PETER HAMMOND

BXQ
5992
. R58

BX
615
.R5
1966

ST. JOSEPH'S UNIVERSITY   STX
BXQ 5992 .R58
Anatomy of a church;

3 9353 00015 8822

FORDHAM UNIVERSITY PRESS

98220

FORDHAM UNIVERSITY PRESS
Bronx, New York 10458

First published 1966

© Mario Rinvolucri 1966

Library of Congress Catalog Card No. : 66-30071

Printed in Great Britain by
Billing & Sons Limited, Guildford and London

Set in Linotype Granjon

To

the People of Zagara

acknowledgements

This book could not have been written without the insight the Boeotian village of Zagara gave me into Greek life. I wish to thank all the Zagarites and especially Morfo and Takis Kiriakatis and Sophia and Taxiarchis Papaioannou whose hospitality and help were unfailing.

I am indebted to people connected with the Church in Sophia, Istanbul, Athens, Salonica and many smaller Greek towns for the help they have given me. Foremost among these are Professor Hamilcar Alivizatos, Fr John Alexiou, Fr Dimitrios Fefes, Fr John Findlow, Fr Paul Garo, Fr Paul Bouchagiar, Fr Anastasios Yannoulatos and Fr John Maddock-Lyon. The list is too long to complete but my gratitude to all is heart-felt.

My thanks are also due to the Editors of *The Tablet* and the *Month* for allowing me to use material already published in these journals.

foreword

FROM 1948 until the spring of 1950 I was living in Greece, and when I returned to England I wrote a book, originally entitled *An Anatomy of the Greek Church*, in which I attempted to give some account of the recent history of an institution which had been almost wholly neglected by English writers since the beginning of the eighteenth century. It was several years before I succeeded in finding a publisher for the book, and when it eventually appeared in 1956 as *The Waters of Marah* it was in some important respects already out of date. It was, however, the only work then available in English which described in some detail and at first hand the life of the contemporary Greek Church; it received some generous reviews and over the next few years acquired a certain modest reputation as a book suitable for reading aloud in the refectories of religious communities during the penitential seasons of the liturgical year. It has been out of print for several years.

I think that *The Waters of Marah* still has some value as a description of the Greek Church at one particular moment in its history, but as an account of "the present state of the Greek Church", to quote its sub-title, it is completely out of date. The world which it describes is the world of the late forties, and much has happened since then, both in Greece and in the Christian world as a whole. Anyone who has been in touch with developments in Greece over the last fifteen years will be aware of the need for a book which takes up where my own earlier essay left off and which analyses the state of the Greek Church in the mid-sixties. Mario Rinvolucri's book does precisely this. It provides the general reader with an inside picture of the Greek Orthodox community which is

clearly based on first-hand experience and a very thorough knowledge of the Greek Church. I know of no other book which traces
the developments of the fifties and early sixties in the Greek
Orthodox world with such perception or discrimination. It also
provides a very interesting and valuable study of attitudes within
the Greek Church towards the wider events which have been
taking place within the Christian world over the last fifteen years,
attitudes which are still only very imperfectly understood by
Western Christians but which are of vital importance for the
future of Orthodox-Catholic *rapprochement* and for the development of a genuine dialogue between the Greek East and the Latin
West.

Mr Rinvolucri has written a most valuable essay. I am privileged
to commend it to the attention not only of the Catholic ecumenist,
for whom it must become required reading, but also to the con-
sideration of all who share the author's concern for the renewal of
the Church and the wiping away of the indifference, suspicion,
enmity, hate and fanaticism which are the legacy of what Professor
Alivizatos calls "the centuries and their harsh happenings".

Peter Hammond

contents

preface

MOST WESTERN conversations about Catholic-Orthodox *rapprochement* centre on historical and theological matters but leave out of account the practical state of affairs inside Orthodoxy today. The high-powered conversations that have been going on for nearly three years in Cardinal Bea's Secretariat for Christian Unity in Rome are exceptions to this. There a panel of experts, whose desks are piled high with the latest Orthodox newspapers and magazines, discuss in detail everything that is going on inside Orthodoxy and how it affects East-West *rapprochement*. The aim of this book is to give the general reader something of the same inside picture of Orthodoxy that the experts in Rome have already undoubtedly built up for themselves.

Orthodoxy today falls into two main divisions: the Slav cycle (plus Rumania) and the Greek cycle. This book describes the latter and in particular the Church of Greece. The reason for choosing Greece is simple. It is the only major Orthodox community in which the researcher can examine Orthodox practice and opinions right down to grass-roots level and be fairly sure that the answers he gets to his questions are not distorted for political reasons. Had I gone to Rumania or Yugoslavia and asked the questions the answers to which form this book, the churchmen there would have been forced into devious replies and the police would, as likely as not, have thrown me out.

The analysis of the Greek situation which follows falls into two parts: firstly a presentation of how each component part of the Greek Church functions (the parish, the diocese, the theological faculty) and secondly an evaluation of what the Greeks at each ecclesiastical level feel about the Western Church and hopes of East-West *rapprochement*. At the end of the book, in Appendix I, the reader will find a report on a brief and necessarily superficial investigation of the Bulgarian Orthodox Church, just to remind him of the existence and importance of the Slav cycle.

This book is not about theology. Being a journalist rather than a theologian I thought it better not to deal specifically with theological questions, except in so far as they are inevitably bound up with discussion of the Greek ecclesiastical situation.

I wrote this book in the summer of 1965 since when Vatican II has concluded its final session and Rome and Constantinople have lifted their mutual excommunications. By the time the Greek theologians had reacted in print to the fourth session of the Vatican Council the book was too far advanced in production for me to add a detailed analysis of their reactions, which, however, were similar to earlier reactions to the first three sessions (see chapter 6).

Though clearly the lifting of excommunications is the first concrete step in Orthodox-Catholic *rapprochement*, until the other Orthodox Churches ratify Constantinople's action it is impossible to estimate its long-term significance. So far (August 1966) only the Church of Cyprus has officially ratified the lifting of the excommunications.

1

the village parish

THE CHURCH of the village of Agia Triada, Boeotia, was full to the doors, the men in front and the women packing the back of the church and the gallery. It was Thursday evening in Holy Week and the village had gathered for the reading of the "Twelve Gospels"[1] which describe Christ's death and entombment. All were standing, for most Orthodox churches only provide stall seats along the walls for the old or infirm. The two cantors were approaching the point where Christ gives up the ghost. Women behind me in the crowd were sobbing audibly. The pappás slowly fixed the base of a wooden cross into an old orange box, kept for this purpose from year to year. Then he lifted a wooden effigy of our Lord and placed it against the cross—there were holes ready in the hands and the feet and corresponding holes in the cross through which two villagers slipped three long nails. A man behind me murmured dryly: *"Páei, stavróthike"* (That's it, they've crucified him). There was nothing emotional about the way he said it—to him it was a dry fact, an immediate reality.

The unquestioning faith of people in Greek villages (half the country's $8\frac{1}{2}$ million population) is something remarked on by all observers. John Campbell, in his excellent study of the Sarakatsan shepherds, writes: "I have met no Sarakatsanos who doubts the existence of God. Such a question seems to them unintelligent. A man takes out his watch and asks: 'Somebody made this watch, is it possible that no one made the world?' "[2] Indeed the question

[1] Twelve passages from the four Gospels.
[2] *Honour, Family and Patronage* (Clarendon Press, Oxford, 1964), p. 322.

never comes up for discussion in the coffee-shops of Greek villages because there is no one to ask it.

The ritual expression of faith, the liturgy, is closely associated in the villagers' minds with the pastoral and agricultural cycle of the year. Time is normally measured in terms of the liturgical year—people refer to when they intend to do things in relation to the feasts of the Church and saints' days: "I'll go and see him on St George's day" or "She'll get married on the second day of the Resurrection" (Easter Bank Holiday). The feasts of the Church are closely associated in people's minds with the most important annual events in their lives: for the shepherd Christmas falls as the first ewes start lambing, while for the peasant farmer the feast of the Twelve Apostles coincides with the wheat harvest. The villagers easily accept and understand the rhythm of the liturgical year, since their own working year closely depends on the rhythm of the seasons. The Orthodox Church's four long fasts (prior to Christmas, Easter, the Twelve Apostles and the Falling asleep of the Virgin [corresponding to the Assumption]) also help to integrate the liturgical cycle of the year into people's lives on a practical level.

True, not many villagers abstain from the proscribed meat, eggs, fish, milk and olive oil for the full month and a bit before Christmas, but even if they do not keep the fast they acknowledge this as a failure and have a sense of guilt. For example, some villagers if caught not fasting by a stranger will excuse themselves.

The only concept of holiday that exists in the villagers' minds is immediately bound up with the feasts of the Church. The time to down tools, kill a lamb, drink, sing and dance is at the next feast in the Church's calendar. Another good excuse for a holiday is a wedding or one of the connected ceremonies like the betrothal or the dowry send-off. Weddings generally take place on a religious feastday and since the couple often come from different villages they offer opportunities for holiday travel and a day's change of environment which it would never occur to a peasant to take for its own sake.

Greek villagers are not themselves aware of being very religious people, and yet, as I have shown, a basically and largely unconsciously religious way of facing situations is common to nearly all of them. Take as a further example the building of a house : when the peasant lays the foundation of a new building he places a bowl of holy water in three of the four corners. All his relations and friends gather and the priest blesses the new foundations. The three bowls are then immured in reinforced concrete and everybody knows that the house has been founded on the symbol of the Holy Trinity. When the time comes for the roof to go on the builders put up a cross roughly made of two scaffolding boards and all the owner's well-wishers come and drape a towel or a handkerchief over the arms of the cross.

The sign of the cross, repeated three times and made with the thumb and first two fingers bunched to symbolize the Trinity, is a normal reaction to a number of everyday situations. All peasants when eating at home make the triple sign of the cross before beginning the meal; as they start on a journey they cross themselves and the women do so every time the bus passes a church or wayside chapel. Campbell writes that the Sarakatsan shepherd out minding his sheep in the hills automatically crosses himself at the approach of danger.

In every peasant house I have ever been into there has been an icon, usually of the Virgin and Child, propped up on a high shelf in the eastern corner of the room; at night the woman of the house lights a little lamp in front of it. At the entrance to a village there is nearly always an "iconostasis", or pillar about the height of an English post-box with an enclosed space at the top for an icon and a wee olive oil lamp.

The a-christian feast of the birthday is unknown in the villages (and in the towns for that matter except for those with pre-christian names like Sophocles and Themistocles). The individual's feast is his nameday when he must stay at home and wait for his relations and friends to come and wish him "many years (of life)". This custom further imprints the cycle of the liturgical year on people's consciousness.

Accepting as they do the supernatural forces of good, especially as personified in the Trinity, Christ and our Lady, to be facts of daily life, Greek country people quite logically also accept the power of the Devil in human affairs. Disorders which do not respond to the local doctor's treatment, often psychologically caused ones, come to be regarded as possession by the Devil and fairly frequent recourse is had to the exorcisms prescribed by the Orthodox Church. One such exorcism is for the priest to divest after Mass, piling his vestments on the head of the afflicted person and saying certain prayers; another is for the Gospel during Mass to be read over the head of the person concerned. Such practices may seem to be founded on ignorance of psychiatric methods but, however this may be, they are a clear indication of a Greek country person's vivid idea of the Devil. Another custom that gives further evidence of this is the invariable habit of adults spitting in a small baby's face when they first see it. The idea is that when a person sees a beautiful new being he will consciously or unconsciously experience envy, the Devil's sin against God, and this may send the baby into a decline. When the person spits and shows visible disgust the evil that would otherwise be caused by envy is averted.

So far we have seen the way in which the village community's basically religious attitudes affect the individual's everyday actions, eating a meal, going on a journey, building a house and so on. The interpenetration of religious and everyday life also works the other way. Two of the Orthodox Church's seven sacraments, marriage and baptism, have acquired an extreme social and material importance in the life of the community in addition to their spiritual significance. Marriage, through the dowry system, has become one of the main ways of inheriting property. Far from dying out, the dowry system in the villages gets stronger year by year as the bridegrooms make more and more ambitious claims on the property of their fathers-in-law. For many men the dowry they get means the possibility of buying more sheep or land, building a shop in a nearby town or migrating to Athens. Marriage also offers the new couple the chance of getting a *koumbáros* (marriage sponsor) with higher social status and greater political influence than their own. Since advancement in Greece largely depends on knowing the right political people the procurement of a suitable *koumbáros* is of great importance. An influential *koumbáros* may mean a loan from the Agricultural Bank, a safe job in government employment, or a place in school for a child. Quite apart from its acknowledged spiritual importance as a sacrament marriage is a turning point in the economic and social life of the Greek villager.

Baptism and confirmation[3] have also acquired considerable social significance. The *koumbáros* normally acts as godfather to the first child, but for subsequent children the parents try to find other godparents with political influence. The relationship of the marriage sponsor and godparents to the family is taken very seriously both on the spiritual and the profane level. On the spiritual level the family and the marriage sponsor's and godparents' families are considered to be related, which precludes intermarriage between them : for example, the godchild may not marry one of his godparent's offspring. On the profane level the godparents and *koumbároi* take their patronage obligations seriously and use their influence all they can to help the family that has thus honoured them.

At least four main things are necessary for a Greek village com-

---

[3] The two sacraments are jointly administered by a priest, not a bishop, between six and eighteen months after the birth of the child.

munity to feel satisfied with itself : a track up to the village from the nearest road, electric light, a school and a church. The track, the electric light and the school are the responsibility of the State and all the villagers can do is to send their representatives to badger the relevant Government authorities. The church, however, is solely their responsibility and as a consequence often becomes a symbol of community pride. In the same way that every male villager must own a respectable dark suit for Sundays and special occasions, so the community must have a presentable church properly decorated with frescoes[4] and icons. Out of sixteen Boeotian villages I investigated, seven had completely new churches and an eighth had renovated its church. In four cases the old churches had been burned down by the Germans as reprisals during the war, but in three cases the villagers had themselves pulled down their old church and built a new one despite the fact that year by year more and more people from their area migrate to Athens.

Very little outside help is available for the building of village churches. The State in a few cases makes a grant from the tax on the National Lottery, and in very poor areas like Epirus the Queen's Fund (a State charitable fund) has helped to put up some of the money needed. The bulk of the money is given by the village people themselves. In one village the 500 families each gave the priest one chicken which he sold against 500 bags of cement. A certain amount of money is raised in lump sums from villagers who have emigrated to the U.S. or Australia, but not all villages can boast a rich *Amerikanós*. Church building expenses are high because few villages are satisfied with the comparatively simple and cheap basilica style. It behoves a village's self-respect to build in the "byzantine" style, which involves a large and expensive central dome. The expenses in bringing a new church into being do

---

[4] I use the term "fresco" loosely, since the paintings on the walls of Greek churches are not often done on wet plaster.

not stop with the building of the shell. Equally necessary is its interior decoration with frescoes. To the Orthodox a church without the head of the Pantocrator in the main dome and a fresco of the Mother and Child in the apse above the altar is quite unfinished. The covering of all the upper part of the main body of the church with frescoes is a heavy charge on the village's economy, as is witnessed by the fact that several years sometimes elapse between the finishing of the shell and the completion of the frescoes.

When a new community comes into being the first thing it does is to build a church. Since 1945 nearly thirty families have trickled down from the hill village of Koroneia to form the new settlement of Agoriani on the main Athens–Levadeia road. In 1961, before they had even managed to get the State to build them a school, they started on a church. The £60 to buy the site were given by an *Amerikanós*. The shell of the little basilica style church was erected by 1964 at a cost of about £2,000. Some of this money came from collections in surrounding villages, but the bulk of it was their own money. It works out at about £60 per family over three years which is a very large amount in the budget of the average peasant household. In 1964 the people of Agoriani still had no priest, but during Holy Week they went each day to light their candles in the church and say a prayer; on Easter Saturday night a pappás from a nearby village "came and did the Resurrection for us". The villagers were delighted to be able to show me their new cemetery with its four freshly laid tombstones : "Now we can bury our dead near to us, instead of taking them up to the old village."

Greek peasants are not only willing to bear the financial burden of building a church for their community; in some cases they are even ready to defy the official Church and the State to this end. In the little 250-family village of Menidi, on the edge of Athens' outer suburbs, the people decided to build themselves a church although they had been refused permission to do so by both the Athens Archbishopric and the Planning Authorities. One Sunday in February 1965 men, women and children worked from dawn to dusk : where in the morning there had only been drums of water and piles of bricks, cement and sand, by seven o'clock in the evening a small church stood on the bare hillside. With the roof half on, the old pappás, who had donated the plot of land for the site, blessed the church and celebrated the first service. Subsequent attempts by police demolition squads to pull the church down were successfully thwarted by the Menidi mothers who locked their children into the building and themselves stood round the outside. The community paid the price of ten of its members standing trial for obstructing the police in the course of their duties, but the church had been built.

The greatest wave of post-war church building has occurred in the villages of Northern Greece where the Germans and Bulgars (1941–44) and the Greek leftists (1946–49) burnt down many of the old churches. The old churches mostly dated from the time of the four-century Turkish occupation (which only ended in Northern Greece in 1913) and even where they were not burnt down they have often had to be replaced because they were too small and dark for the present needs of the villages. Under the Turks it had not been prudent to build ostentatiously.

We have spoken of the peasants and the village churches, but what of the priests? Perhaps the best way to give some idea of the life of a Greek rural priest is to outline how one of them runs his parish. Fr George, who ministers to the 750–soul parish of Ippsilanti, Boeotia, is an example of the best type of village priest. His busy day in the week is Sunday, which he starts by singing matins and the Mass. The combined service begins at 6.30 a.m. and ends around 9.30. The people start coming at 8.30 when the priest has got as far as the Gospel. In the course of the year most of the congregation are women and children, but at Christmas and Easter the men turn out in force and about half of the village's adult population take Holy Communion. At other times of the year it is rare to see villagers communicating, except when mothers bring their babies to their first communion which happens a few months after the baptism-confirmation ceremony. The Orthodox Church does not rule that attendance at Mass every Sunday is mandatory on all the faithful and people have no feeling of guilt if they miss a Sunday or two. Fr George's congregation is at its lowest in the peak agricultural periods like June and July when the villagers work a seven-day week harvesting the wheat and weeding the cotton, and in the coldest periods of winter when people prefer their draughty houses to an even draughtier and colder church. After Mass Fr George goes over to the village square and chats for a while in one of the coffee-shops (the coffee-shop, a sort of all-male club, is the central social institution of the village). He then goes home for lunch and siesta, followed at 3 p.m. by a catechism class for the three top forms of the local elementary school. The day I attended the class Fr George was annoyed because only thirty-five of the fifty-five children who ought to have come turned up. The lesson that day was about the birth of Christ as the shepherds saw it, and the priest's skilful choice of angle obviously gripped his class, many of whose fathers are shepherds. During the week the priest sings vespers each day and attends to any other jobs that have to be done, such as visiting the sick, issuing various certificates, and the like.

I asked Fr George if in his view the priest has a responsibility for his flock beyond the celebration of Mass and the signing of birth, marriage and death certificates. He replied that the priest could nourish people's spiritual lives in two ways : (i) directly, by regularly preaching a sermon that draws the practical moral from the Gospel of the day; (ii) indirectly, by drawing the conversation in the coffee-shop round to discussing whether certain of the villagers' actions are right or wrong. He said the second method could have great influence because it put social pressure on wrong-doers to amend.

Fr George, with a small parish, has plenty of time to supervise the cultivation of his fields in his nearby native village. The money from his land and his £21 13s. a month salary as a second-class priest (see below) enable him to maintain one of the most presentable houses in the village and to live very adequately. He is a family man (as all parish priests are by tradition supposed to be) and has married off one of his daughters to a respectable clerk in a nearby market town. The arguments in favour of parish priests being married are that they are less likely to lead immoral lives and that they find it easier to integrate into the life of the village when they have a normal family like everybody else. In addition, if a priest has a good wife she can help him understand certain of the problems of women parishioners that, as a man, he might not otherwise fully understand.

The upkeep of the church at Ippsilanti is in the hands of a committee of four villagers (proposed by the priest and appointed by the bishop). They collect the money from the sale of candles and part of the money paid for ceremonies (marriages, etc.) and this they use to pay the running expenses of the church : the £4 per month paid to the two cantors and the bills for cleaning, electricity and minor repairs. Major repairs are paid for by a collection in the village and at such times even the poorest people make an effort to contribute.

Fr George is a second-class priest, which means that he has had a secondary education and two years at a major seminary. Although he is not a first-class or theologian priest (four years' university theology) he has enough of a general formation and sufficient theological knowledge to preach on Sundays and hold sensible catechism classes. Unfortunately very few priests in the Boeotian diocese of Thebes and Levadeia are in this category. The diocese has :

80 parish priests, of whom :

0 are first class
8 are second class (like Fr George)
57 are third class
15 are fourth class.

The third-class priests have had a couple of years secondary education and then a year or two at a minor seminary. Their seminary time was often as much as ten years and more after leaving school. In the late 1950s the minor seminaries were brought up to the standards of the major seminaries, in theory at least; this involved a change of curriculum and in some cases of teachers. They began taking only boys with a full secondary education. To-day, therefore, minor seminaries have ceased to exist and no more third-class priests are being turned out.

The fourth and final class consists of priests ordained under the old semi-democratic system by which the village elders chose a suitable young man and sent him to the bishop. After a few weeks' catechizing and instruction in how to take the various services, the bishop would ordain the village's nominee a priest. Many of these fourth-class priests have never even finished elementary school. This system finally went out with the war and the fourth-class priests are now mostly old men.

What the above statistics add up to is that the 115,000 people living in the Thebes and Levadeia diocese have no parish priests who, educationally speaking, could possibly have been admitted to Anglican or Catholic orders. The picture in this diocese is averagely depressing. Going down the scale we have the see of Didimoticho on the Turkish border with :

84 parish priests, of whom :

1 is first class
10 are second class
31 are third class
42 are fourth class.

(Thus, exactly half of the priests in the diocese of Didimoticho have only been to elementary school.)

Going up the scale, we have the diocese of Volos (Dimitriados) with :

> 138 parish priests, of whom :
> 8 are first class
> 65 are second class
> 35 are third class
> 30 are fourth class.

To return to Boeotia, what strikes one most in touring the villages is not the average priest's lack of education, for which statistics have prepared one, but his lack of spirituality. In contrast with the even less educated monks the average village pappás is remarkably poverty-stricken spiritually. He normally thinks of his life in terms of his wife and family, his land and his "job" which he performs and for which he is paid like any other village official, such as the secretary or the *garde-champêtre*. I asked one priest whose parish is a village twelve miles from Thebes, but who lives all the week in Thebes, if he did not think it was odd, a priest living away from his flock. He replied : "Oh, you mean wouldn't it be better if I had a parish here in Thebes? Yes, the Bishop has promised me that as soon as one falls vacant he'll let me have it!" Even the young second-class priests fresh from the seminary often have a hard, professional attitude to their ecclesiastical duties rather than a vocational one. When visiting village priests you rarely disturb them in their spiritual reading because few of them ever do read or meditate. Do they go to confession regularly? In general I cannot say, but one old priest I asked told me he had last been three years before.

The root of the problem of lack of spirituality among village priests lies in the selection of the seminary candidates and in the seminaries themselves. Since there are 700 parishes without priests in Northern Greece alone the seminaries are not fussy as to whom they take in as long as the candidate has had a full secondary education. The dimensions of the seminary courses are not conducive to the cultivation of either scholarship or spirituality. For two years the seminarian spends forty hours a week on a school bench listening to an unending spate of information on sixteen different subjects. I have attended a full day of these classes and in most of them the pupils make no active contribution whatsoever either in the form of question-asking during the class or written exercises after the class. They are never required to prepare for a lesson, only to memorize what the teacher said the time before. They are not required to do any reading of their own. They do all the subjects in the University theology curriculum plus ten hours a week learning about specifically priestly duties, plus several hours devoted to agriculture, medical care and music. The result of this monstrous programme, all to be got through in two years, is that seminarians retain little of what they have heard and leave the seminary as untrained to think as when they arrived. The saddest thing is that the weight of this half-useless study leaves no time over for seminarians to learn to pray or meditate, and into the bargain these things are not taught systematically. The deplorable state of Greece's ten main seminaries goes a long way towards explaining the lack of spirituality among the rural parish clergy.

Parish priests are paid State salaries according to their class. Their salaries per month work out at:

> First class: £26 0s. 0d.
> Second class: £21 13s. 0d.
> Third class: £18 10s. 0d.
> Fourth class: £15 5s. 0d.

Five per cent of their salary is deducted at source to finance a pension fund. The pension is half the salary. There are about 500 first-class priests in Greece of whom 220 are parish priests, about

1,500 second-class priests, while the remaining 6,000 are either third- or fourth-class. All priests in villages with 1,500 souls or less get a monthly bonus of about £6. Because Northern Greece does not produce enough priests of her own, southerners have to be enticed North with a 50 per cent bonus on their salaries. Not many of them go, for all that. The frontier diocese of Kilkis in Macedonia has forty out of 141 villages without a priest as well as seventeen hamlets of less than 200 people in like condition. Fourteen of the forty vacant parishes had lost their parish priest five or more years before the time of my enquiry (early 1965). As a result one priest in this diocese may have as many as five scattered mountain villages in his care.

Besides his salary a priest has his *tichurá*, or luck-money, from baptisms, marriages, holy unctions, funerals, requiems, house-blessings, and so on. In certain areas it can hardly be called luck-money any more since the bishopric has gone so far as to fix a rate. In a village in the see of Kilkis you pay : £2 7s. for a baptism, £2 14s. for a wedding, £1 18s. for a funeral, £1 9s. for a requiem. (Half the fee goes to the priest and the other half pays various taxes and is used for the upkeep of the church.) In a reasonably prosperous parish in Boeotia luck-money may increase the priest's monthly income by about £10, but it all depends on the size and wealth of the community. There are villages in Greece where luck-money is almost nil.

Apart from his salary and perks the village priest often has land he can cultivate. In the previously-mentioned enquiry into sixteen Boeotian parishes ten of the priests were native and owned land in the village and three had land in a nearby village. Apart from salary, luck-money and revenue from the land a few country priests find other ways of increasing their incomes. In one Boeotian village the priest is the local telephone exchange operator and gets 30 per cent of the price paid for each of the outgoing calls; he also runs a van-cum-taxi which brings in the money he needs to educate his five children and provide dowries for his daughters. Despite the above picture of comparative affluence, at any rate by village standards, there are still priests in certain areas who live in dire poverty and their families with them.

How does the generally low level of education and spirituality of the country clergy affect the villagers of Greece who, as we have seen, have a basically religious outlook on life? One answer is that in the sixteen Boeotian villages the average church attendance on normal Sundays is only 6 per cent of the population.[5] The proportion of women to men is at least two to one in any normal Sunday congregation even though the women cook, bake bread, see to their children as well as weeding and picking the cotton and reaping the wheat where the harvester cannot go. In a quarter of the sixteen villages church attendance is considerably higher than the average and it is significant that in these four villages the parish priests are more spiritually aware men than most of their colleagues.

Greeks, somewhat like Irishmen, have a great respect for the ability to use words, and undoubtedly the prospect of a well-delivered sermon would draw some of them to church. One café owner told me that it would be better if the village had a good priest. Asked what he meant, he said: "A man who'd take pleasure in saying a couple of words in church or in the café."

[5] This estimate is based on figures suggested by the parish priests themselves and on personal observation over a period of two years. The 6 per cent does not include the elementary school children who are marshalled by the teacher and marched into church, the boys in one platoon and the girls in another.

It is reported in a recent study (*The Internal Migrant*, Moustaka, Athens, 1965) that 80 per cent of a sample of migrants to Athens from the Zagori area in Epirus and from the island of Paros declared that they used to go to church regularly every Sunday when they lived in their villages. Dr Moustaka's migrants were clearly idealizing their former church-going habits since evidence from World Council of Churches workers in Epirus villages tallies with my own findings in Boeotia, that the average church attendance on a normal Sunday would be between 5 and 10 per cent of the population of the parish.

Another thing that keeps Greeks in the villages away from church is a priest who celebrates Mass shoddily, has a bad singing voice, or some other defect of this type. However, the main reason for low church attendance is the parish priest's lack of personal spirituality.

Do villagers go to confession and communion? Traditionally the Orthodox are meant to go to communion, preceded by confession, at Easter, the Twelve Apostles, the Falling asleep of the Virgin (Assumption) and Christmas. Let us take the case of Agios Giorgios, one of the four villages with a spiritual priest. Fr Seraphim says that at Easter half the people in the village (population 2,300) go to communion but that not more than 150 people come to him for confession,[6] and of these not more than twenty are men. Given that the Orthodox Church requires the faithful to purge their souls through confession before taking communion, why do so few people in the village go? Fr Seraphim suggested three reasons. Firstly, people don't like telling their secrets to somebody they and everybody else in the village know well. They are afraid that the secrecy of the confessional may not be respected. Secondly, some people think they can tell their sins to the icon of the Mother and Child and so be forgiven without recourse to a priest. Thirdly, young couples don't want to see the confessor because they want small families and use the "safe period", while the priest tells them they should have a minimum of four children. A further major reason why people do not go to confession to the village priest is because, though they get absolution, they do not get satisfactory advice on how to solve their particular problems. The priest simply does not have the intellectual formation necessary to grasp and offer solutions to the problems he listens to in the confessional.

The Church of Greece has taken certain steps to supply the deficiencies of her rural clergy as preachers and confessors. In each

---

[6] Not all parish priests are allowed to hear confessions. Out of the eighty priests in the Thebes and Levadeia diocese only thirty are confessors.

diocese there is at least one first-class priest whose exclusive job it is to preach, take catechism classes and hear confessions. He has no parish. In the diocese of Thebes and Levadeia, for example, there are two theologian priests and one lay preacher doing this work. They are responsible for the ninety-three parishes,[7] which means that in theory each village should be visited on a Sunday or a feast-day at least once in the year. This does not quite work out, how-ever, since the preachers have to concentrate on the larger villages and on communities where the faith is felt to be in special danger, for example a place with an Evangelical minority or where half the villagers are leftists. Because of this and their relative in-accessibility many smaller hill villages may go eighteen months or two years without having a sermon.

The universal experience of such preachers is that the villagers are eager to have the Gospel explained. They crowd out the church or coffee-shop to listen to a sermon. Few preachers can spare the time from preaching to hear confessions, but several of them have told me that if they could stay as long as there was a queue outside the confessional in many villages two-thirds of the population would come to confession. Since it is not possible for enough first-class priests to visit the villages and hear confessions, the Church of Greece from 1957 on has organized intensive two-month courses the aim of which is to turn country priests into adequate con-fessors. Between 1957 and 1964 some 600 priests had taken the course, which is run by some of Greece's best confessors and University teachers of theology. The priests, of all ages and drawn from parishes all over the country, spend two months in an atmo-sphere of lively intellectual retreat in the peaceful Pendeli monas-tery near Athens. The classes are conducted in the colloquial language and plenty of time is allowed for question and answer work. My impression after a day spent attending the course was

[7] In late 1964 the Thebes and Levadeia diocese had thirteen vacant parishes —hence the discrepancy between eighty priests and ninety-three parishes.

that some of these often elderly third- and fourth-class priests were being given real spiritual training for the first time in their lives. They were clearly finding it extremely invigorating. To this extent the confessors' course is of great importance, but whether the priests, on returning to their villages, find more people coming to confession is another story.

What do the villagers think of their pappás, who has little more education than his peasant contemporaries and often much less than the young men who have been to school since 1949? The image of the village priest as a grabbing, uneducated, clownish figure may exist in upper-class Athenian drawing-rooms, but in the villages anti-clericalism is rare, even in leftist areas. However bad a priest may be, the villagers respect his office which is part of the divinely ordained way things are. For example, in one of the sixteen Boeotian villages there is a priest who is so slack that he does not even say Sunday Mass regularly. One Sunday he was away in the local town; another, he had none of the special bread required for the Eucharist; and on a third he complained that nobody would bring him wood to heat the church. When I suggested that he should go out with an axe and a mule and cut some wood himself, as the other peasants do, my suggestion was met with disapproval by the villagers who were sitting round us in the café. One old man said : "No, we wouldn't like the pappoúli to go out himself and cut wood for the church; the reason why we don't do things for him readily is because he's always grousing at us." Even though the village has been saddled with this inadequate priest for fifteen years, they still respect his office and his right as parish priest to be helped by the community. The sad result of his inadequacy is that even when he gets round to saying Mass, almost nobody goes. He is a man of fifty and in good health.

After an examination of Greek village parishes one is left with an impression of fine leaven but poor bakers, of a religious people, but of educationally and, above all, spiritually inadequate pastors.

ECUMENICAL ATTITUDES IN THE VILLAGE PARISHES

The simple peasant farmer regards himself as a Christian and, if asked to be more precise, as an Orthodox Christian. When someone comes along and claims to be a Christian but not an Orthodox the average country Greek concludes that he is talking through his hat. If you are a Christian you are an Orthodox—it's the same thing. Side by side with this notion that Christian equals Orthodox is the idea he has absorbed from the newspapers that all the Christian Churches are working towards reunion. He is therefore vaguely aware that the Protestants and Catholics claim to be Christians too. The average Greek peasant knows little about the Reformation Churches but is somewhat more aware of the claims and teaching of the Catholic Church (see ecumenical section in Chapter 2). The Greek villagers' discussions of ecumenical[8] matters are usually prompted by front-page news stories like the Pope-Patriarch meeting in the Holy Land (January 1964) or the return by the Vatican of the skull of the Apostle Andrew to Patras (September 1964). His four main sources of knowledge for discussing such matters are: (i) memories of history classes at school in which he learnt about the misdeeds of the later crusaders (1204 and onwards); (ii) memories of catechism classes in which he learnt about the "errors" of the Roman Church;[9] (iii) information gleaned from the newspapers and (iv) whatever he may pick up in the way of information or attitude from the village priest. The average peasant has only a dim recollection of what he learnt from the first two sources which presented him with information about the Catho-

[8] In the course of the book the adjective "ecumenical" will be used in two senses: (i) to mean "connected with the relations of various separated Christian Churches": e.g. the Pope-Patriarch meeting was an ecumenical event of great importance; (ii) to mean "favourable or well disposed towards the *rapprochement* of the Churches": e.g. "an ecumenical-attitude".

[9] For a summary of the differences between Catholic and Orthodox teaching and practice see Appendix II.

lic Church under a definitely hostile light. In recent years, when
the papers have covered Catholic affairs, the coverage has been on
the whole sympathetic—most Greek papers have come out editori-
ally in favour of moves towards a *rapprochement* of the Churches.

What the Greek villager learns from his parish priest is more
difficult to assess. Given the generally low standard of education
of the clergy, the average country priest *knows* little more than his
flock about ecumenical matters. It is possible to distinguish three
attitudes among the country clergy. The majority take a defensive
and rather negative stand summed up in the pithy words of one
fourth-class priest: "The Catholics will have to come over to us.
Let us take an example : this glass is whole and sound"—picking
up a glass from the café table—"the other has a crack in it. Will
the sound glass have to be cracked for there to be union?" Another
point of view often heard in one form or other from country
priests is this : "Those gentlemen the Catholics are obstinate—they
are determined to stick to their errors, like the infallibility of the
Pope and the mistaken view of the Trinity (*filioque*)." (Orthodoxy
teaches that the Holy Spirit proceeds from the Father only.) Unfortunately the Greek villager often picks up from his parish priest
quite the wrong idea about what the Catholics believe. Many
priests are convinced that papal infallibility, for instance, implies
that the Pope cannot commit a sin ! A second attitude to be found
among a few country priests is apathy about ecumenical questions :
"What have we to do with the Catholics, anyway?" one eighty-
year-old priest asked me. A third and more hopeful attitude is to
be found among some of the young second-class priests who
have just recently left the seminary. Fr Michaïl of Distomo in
Boeotia told me that in the event of an Orthodox-Catholic dialogue,
which he very much hopes will come about, both sides must be
willing to give ground. He suggested the Catholics start off by
ceding on some of the papal claims, while the Orthodox should be
ready to add not *filioque* (from the Son) to the Creed, but a com-

promise clause "through the Son". As younger, better educated priests gradually replace the 6,000 third- and fourth-class priests, the negative and defensive attitudes of the village clergy are likely to be slowly replaced by an attitude at least open to ecumenical developments if not necessarily enthusiastic about them.

In discussions on ecumenical matters Greek country people often cling to their simple fundamentalist faith; for instance, they cannot understand when one suggests that the *filioque* is not as deep and radical a difference between Orthodoxy and Catholicism as it might seem at first sight. They say that if the Catholics claim that the Holy Spirit proceeds from the Father and the Son, well, they are absolutely wrong, and that is that. Yet in the villages of Boeotia I have heard men in the coffee-shops arguing almost equally for and against reunion. Those in favour say that it is a crying shame that half a dozen differences should keep the Orthodox and Catholics apart when the vast bulk of their faith is identical. Those against object that since the Catholics refuse to understand the true nature of the Trinity, fail to baptize their children (only pouring water instead of complete immersion), only half communicate (bread but no wine), and finally believe that a man (the Pope) is infallible, then there is nothing much that can profitably be said to them.

What would be the reaction of the Greek peasant farmers to an eventual theological and organizational *modus vivendi* between the two Churches? Two psychological factors would be involved, their conservatism and their *egoïsmós*. If reunion were presented as an innovation or involved changing traditionally held beliefs or even customs there would certainly be villages where a bishop responsible for the act of reunion would be locked out of the church. An example of the simple people's ferocious conservatism in religious matters is the way the old calendar adherents split off from the official Church in 1924.[10]

[10] In 1924 the Church of Greece followed the State's example and dropped

B

If reunion with the Catholics could in any way be interpreted as capitulation or submission to Rome this would at once offend the collective *egoïsmós* of the peasant farmers. *Egoïsmós* is regarded as a virtue especially vital to the male—it includes the notions of self-esteem and honour. The negative power of the *Laós*, the people, must be taken very seriously in any discussion of Orthodox–Catholic *rapprochement*. In Orthodoxy the people are considered to be the ultimate *defensores fidei*. If they are not prepared for reunion by a gradual process of unblinkering and enlightenment it will be reunion only on paper, at least as far as the Greek countryside is concerned.

---

the old Julian Calendar for the new Gregorian Calendar, the calendar of the West. A whole section of the population, led by their priests, reacted against this innovation. By the early 1930s the old calendarists had acquired a hierarchy of their own and had set up a rival archbishop to the official one. The old calendar hierarchy quarrelled and split in the late thirties so that today there are two hierarchies, two Synods and two separate budgets. There are still about 200,000 old calendarists in Greece ministered to by rather less than 250 priests. They refuse to go to Mass in a new calendar church or receive the sacraments from a new calendar pappás. The simple people who follow the old calendar have a fanatical belief in the importance of the thirteen days that separate their liturgical cycle from that of the official, new calendar Church. One old calendar priest told me : "There is a kingdom on earth and a kingdom in heaven. If we went by the new calendar the feast of St Charalambos, for instance, would be celebrated on earth thirteen days earlier than in heaven." The assumption is that heaven is old calendar! Their fanaticism also extends to the ecumenical sphere. In 1961 the *Mattheos* group of old calendarists published a particularly vicious pamphlet entitled *Papism the Anti-Christ*, of which this is a typical extract: "Papism the sadistic, relentless enemy of Orthodoxy, Papism the implacable adversary of the Byzantine Empire and the Greek race, Papism responsible for the dissolution of the Byzantine Empire, for the fall of Constantinople, for four centuries of slavery, for the parcelling out of the Greek inheritance. . . ." Though the old calendarists are out of step with the majority in Greece, in terms of world Orthodoxy they are in step, since the largest Orthodox group, the Slavs, have also retained the old calendar.

2
the town parish

IN CONSIDERING the question of the town parishes the first step is to determine what is meant by "town". Greece has two great cities, Athens in the south and Salonica in the north, which between them account for more than a quarter of the country's eight and a half million people. Athens' population has grown in recent years to two million and Salonica now has a population of 400,000. The third town in Greece, Patras, has a population of only about 100,000 and comes at the head of a quite different class of urban community to the city class mentioned above. There are some twenty-five or so provincial towns like Patras with populations ranging between 20,000 and 70,000. They are administrative centres for the surrounding villages, which the peasants visit every so often on business, to do shopping, to sell produce, and so on. Except for one or two central ones round the Cathedral, most parishes in provincial towns broadly correspond to the pattern described in the previous chapter. The people in any given parish tend to know each other, many of them being related; the men meet in the local coffee-shops and there is a sense of community, even if not as tight as in the village. When a peasant migrates from a village into one of these towns he modifies his pattern of living but is not forced into completely new patterns, as he would be if he migrated to the vast conurbations of Athens or Salonica. The priest is still a familiar figure to be met socially in the coffee-shop, a man of the people among the people.

But not more than one-eighth of the population of Greece lives in these provincial towns—the great, post-war migratory explosion has burst over Athens and Salonica. A survey made by the

35

National Statistics Service of Greece shows that between 1952 and 1962, 59 per cent of the migration from the four villages studied was to Athens and only 15 per cent to the other towns. Some of this 15 per cent will have been to Salonica. The four villages picked were in different parts of the country. Nearly half the migrants were found to be under twenty-five years old and their reason for going to Athens was to look for work in the city. One may safely generalize from the findings of the survey and visualize a city of two million people of whom a sizeable percentage are young, half-settled villagers trying to fit into new and difficult surroundings.

Given the sense of community observable in Greek villages, one would expect the migrants from a village to form a colony in one particular area of Athens, but this is not in fact the case. In 1963 there were sixty-five people from the 400-strong Boeotian village of Zagara living in Athens. Only eighteen of these (five families) lived together in a sort of colony in one district. The remaining forty-seven lived in widely scattered suburbs of the city, locations determined mainly by their place of work and in two or three cases by considerations of housing prestige. I observed these migrants closely during the first half of 1963 and it was clear that those living in one remote suburb had little or no contact with those living elsewhere. What contact there was would be at great religious festivals when many of the migrants would return to Zagara to see their relatives. Thus contact came mainly through the original village community, and not through visiting between unrelated families in Athens. This break-up of the closely-knit pattern of village life has been the experience not merely of sixty-five peasants from a little Boeotian village but of most of the 850,000 people who have moved into the capital since 1940.

What effect does his uprooting have on the religious life of the migrant? Instead of belonging to a parish of 500–3,000 souls ministered by one priest, he is thrown into a parish with 5,000–

15,000 faithful looked after by up to four priests. He is unlikely to come into contact with the priests of the parish unless he has to obtain a certificate or arrange for a ceremony. Often migrants arrange for ceremonies like weddings and christenings to take place in their home villages, thus avoiding even bureaucratic contact with the priests of the suburban parish. The only contact many suburban parishioners have with their pastors is seeing them through a sea of heads on an odd Sunday morning.

In the village each family has normally made some gift to the church, an icon, a chandelier, something which to them is distinctive. This attaches each individual, through his family, to the church. The migrant has none of this feeling on entering a large suburban church in Athens—the gifts were made before he arrived and anyway he would not have been able to give enough to pay for anything significant in the church. In the village the church is the community symbol and the villagers have a sense of belonging, whereas in the city the migrants are not integrated into a real community and so do not experience this proprietary feeling in their suburban church.

In the village a committee of four local men is responsible for the business connected with the church. If there are no logs ready to put in the church stove on a winter's Sunday morning the four *"epítropoi"* are criticized in no uncertain fashion by the men in the coffee-shops after Mass. In this way the village really runs its church through a kind of direct parliamentary process, with the coffee-shop as the House of Commons. In an Athenian parish of 10,000 souls with a church council of up to eight laymen there is precious little contact between them and the other parishioners. In a suburban parish the *"epítropoi"* are likely to be from the upper educational and social strata which effectively cuts them off from ordinary social contact with the peasant migrant. (There may be a patronage relationship.) The migrant will certainly have no feeling of being "in" on the running of parish affairs.

The rhythm of life in city suburbs is not exclusively centred round the liturgical calendar, as it is in the village. The main festivals are of course kept, but they no longer have the intimate connection with people's work cycle that they had in the village. For the town Greeks religious feasts fall at various intervals providing welcome holidays extra to the fifty-two Sundays of the year, but they no longer constitute landmarks in the working year around which all social life is organized. Religious feasts have greater significance in the village setting, which is one of the reasons why so many migrants return to celebrate them in their communities of origin. The best example of this is Easter with its mass exodus from Athens and Salonica back to the villages. Bus routes that normally carry a two-hourly service have vehicles leaving every quarter of an hour in the second half of Holy Week. There are of course other factors than religious ones involved in the Easter exodus, but that so many of the migrants go back to their villages at Easter, the great community festival of Greece, is a measure of the failure of the suburban parishes to integrate them and provide a real feeling of community.

When a migrant arrives in Athens or Salonica he finds for the first time that he is free from the moral restraint imposed on him since childhood by the village community. (In the case of young men their two years' military service is a partly comparable period of emancipation from village morality.) Everybody in a village knows everybody else and since nearly all the male villagers spend some part of the day in one of the coffee-shops, a reprobate action, if noticed, never passes without comment. According to village custom, for example, a boy may not talk to a girl unrelated to him; if he does it is immediately known in every household. Being aware of this the boy is correspondingly careful. The village community, through its insatiable curiosity and open criticism, plays a morally preventative part in the life of each of its members. When the villager comes to work in Athens and lives isolated from members of his original community, most of these restrictions vanish. He is free to act according to his own conscience and is no longer necessarily bound by the sanctions and values of the village. There is a danger that the individual trained to observe the rules of a small community may fail to build up a personal morality when he finds himself cut off from that community, particularly as the city life is likely to make him feel that village values are backward and old-fashioned. It is just at this juncture, when spiritual and moral guidance should be forthcoming, that he finds himself lost in a large suburban parish in which the priest is often inaccessible.

Another effect of mass migration into the two big cities has been the exposure of the migrants to agnostic ideas and religious apathy. Fifteen per cent of the Greek electorate regularly votes for the leftist party E.D.A. (United Democratic Left). E.D.A. includes Communists, socialists and liberals with left-wing tendencies, but the Communists are the backbone of the party. Though in most villages there are people who fought for or sympathized with the leftists in the 1946-49 civil war it is difficult to be openly E.D.A. in a Greek village today, unless the majority of the village is leftist. Community feeling in most villages makes allegiance to the party defeated in the civil war a precarious business and life is made difficult for the E.D.A. sympathizer by the Agricultural Bank, the police and the local authorities. As a result it is in the cities that E.D.A.'s influence is strongest. The Communists have not recently pushed the atheistic line nor attacked the Church head-on—they merely try to present religion as a matter of secondary importance beside the crying social injustices apparent everywhere in the country. Typical were the views of a leftist water-vendor in the Athenian suburb of Glyphada on the Gospel: "No one," he told me, "expects you to believe all the stuff you read about God up there in heaven, but Christ certainly left a wonderful social code. . . ."

Another Communist line is to point to the deficiencies of the clergy, to reports of their immorality, to their lack of education, zeal, etc., and so try to alienate people from them. The large, inchoate city suburb where the priest is not personally known by the people is ideal ground for such propaganda.

What are parish priests in suburban Athens doing about the inrush of peasants from traditional village communities all over Greece? A small handful of Athens parish priests have understood the nature of the problem facing them and have a sufficiently vocational attitude to do something about it. Though they are a tiny minority, these priests deserve careful attention since their action illustrates the difficulties of keeping religion meaningful in the new city setting in which half the Greeks will be living by the 1980s. (It has been calculated that if the present rate of in-migration continues, Athens alone will have a population of three and a half million in twenty years.)

The parish of St Stilianos in the Athenian suburb of Ghizi is in the hands of one of these active priests. Fr John Antonopolou, with two priests helping him, runs this mainly working-class parish of 12,000 souls. A large percentage of his parishioners are in-migrants. He himself is a university graduate in theology as is his second in command. The third priest is second class. By Athenian parish standards these three men constitute a team of more than average education. Fr John's work falls into three categories: (i) minimal priestly duties; (ii) evangelization of the parish and (iii) social work.

(i) He says Mass each Sunday, sees that vespers are sung each evening, administers the sacraments and takes his turn every third week (in a parish with three priests) in the church office, seeing parishioners for two hours in the morning and for two hours in the evening. As a confessor he listens to the parish's sins once a week and in the days leading up to Easter he spends days on end in the confessional. Fulfilment of these duties entitles him to draw his State salary as a graduate priest of the first class. He need do no more as far as his "job" of being a priest is concerned.

(ii) Evangelization of the parish : Fr John has organized a wide circle of lay men and women to teach Sunday school classes, run Bible study groups and to visit homes where religion has fallen into disuse. The priests themselves rarely visit because, according to Fr John, they are afraid of falling into morally compromising situations—in fact socio-religious visiting by Greek priests is not a recognized habit. If a priest calls on a family he must have a more precise reason for doing so than just to have a probing chat. Fr John regularly distributes religious pamphlets to the families in the parish. These pamphlets, which he writes himself and has printed, deal with practical questions and doubts such as : "Why should I go to church?", a thought that must often trouble the villager in Athens who misses the warmth of his own small community. The pamphlets are short and to the point; they are written in clear colloquial Greek. During the winter months a series of sermons is preached in St Stilianos in such a way that the ideas of one Sunday follow on to the next and the series forms a whole. Like the pamphlets the sermons are couched in clear, colloquial language, not in the beautiful, but to the people only half comprehensible, "pure" language of the intellectuals. (Most of the priests trained since the war accept the colloquial language as the best vehicle of instruction—it is only in some rural areas of Greece and among the older preachers that the use of the "pure" language persists.) With an almost Don Camillo-like touch Fr John has fitted loudspeakers to the belfries of his hill-top church so that even those who stay in bed on Sunday morning will willy-nilly be aware that Mass is in progress. Being vitally concerned with the lack of suitable young men for the Orthodox priesthood, he has got into contact with the local elementary school teachers so that through their eyes he may spot possible vocations. In early 1964 he told me there were five boys in the elementary schools of Ghizi

who were potential candidates for the priesthood. He makes sure
that special attention is paid to their religious formation and when
the time is ripe he sounds out their parents.

Fr John's third main field of activity is social work. In the spring
of 1963 he organized a week for the poor of the parish—food was
given out at the church door to those who needed it and a number
of lay people took in children from the poorest families for a week.
In this way a lasting link was formed between a number of the
poorest and of the more well-to-do families in the parish. Fr John's
dream is to build a three-storey community centre so as to make
the church the focal point in the Ghizi area. The ground floor he
plans as kitchens and dining rooms to give a midday meal to
children going to elementary school and to feed destitute adults.
The first floor will be baths and a lecture hall and the second floor
will house a library, reading room, records and games room. To
raise money for the centre Fr John has suggested that all the
parishioners with relatives in America should ask them to send as
much money as they can. He himself has appealed to Archbishop
Iakovos, leader of the one and a half million Greek Orthodox in
America, for help and has received the assurance that if he goes
to the U.S. he will be introduced to the biggest Greek businessmen
out there. The sum to be raised is $50,000 (about £17,860).

Fr John of St Stilianos is an outstanding example of a suburban
parish priest who combines three qualities: enthusiasm, a clear
understanding on the intellectual level of the problems of a city
parish, and the practical know-how required to get done the things
he decides ought to be done. He and a handful of other priests
have realized that if the Church is to keep her grip on the new
arrivals in the city she must make herself interested in their present
well-being as well as in their eternal salvation. Hence the development on an equal footing of social work aimed at making the
parish into a coherent community and of modern techniques for
putting across the Gospel message.

The idea of forming a real Christian community in a town parish has been carried even further by Fr George Pirounakis (a university graduate in theology) in the borough of Eleusis, thirteen miles from the centre of Athens. (The site of the ancient Demeter–Persephone mysteries has now grown into a thriving industrial complex with a population of 15,000, producing olive oil, soap and steel.)

In Fr Pirounakis's parish there are 7,000 people and he has two priests helping him. He has organized a lay committee which takes a regular monthly collection in the town and uses the money to provide a warm midday meal for the 200 poorest people there : these include old people without families to support them, cripples, unemployed, etc. Another lay committee organizes an evening meal for the teenagers who work in factories all day and then attend night school from 6 to 10 p.m. Fr Pirounakis has opened a second-hand clothing counter so that the poorest people don't catch cold in the winter.

He has told me that this work is not just personal philanthropy on his part and on the part of certain well-intentioned parishioners. The Christian community as a whole, the parish, has a collective responsibility for its destitute members. Fr Pirounakis feels that the role of the parish priest is to give pastoral guidance in areas of human activity as diverse as industrial relations, ecumenism, politics, and so on. For example, he once persuaded workers who had decided to strike that a hunger strike would further their cause more effectively than an ordinary down-tools. He sees the priest as an up-to-date version of the old ethnarch, the leader of the community in every sphere. Fr Pirounakis has none of Fr John's reservations about visiting people in their homes. He has often been able to mediate in family quarrels and help save marriages from foundering. In one case a poor woman came to him in despair because her husband, having gambled all his money away, had lost their house at the card table. Fr Pirounakis quickly found the necessary money to buy back the house and thus, at least temporarily, saved the marriage.

All this activity and Fr Pirounakis's defence of the workers' justified claims against the local industrialists, still so nineteenth-century in mentality that they refuse to meet the trade union leaders over wage disputes, have frequently drawn down on him the enmity of the civil authorities. In June 1964, their opposition reached such a pitch that he resigned from being parish priest of Eleusis. Many of his parishioners, but not the industrialists, hope that he will return. He has been accused of fraud, of being a Communist and more besides—he is no stranger to the defendant's box in the courts. Fr Pirounakis feels that his is one of the first adequate attempts to solve the problems of the industrial parish and that if the experiment is to be of any use as a prototype it must be given publicity. Accordingly he has written and spoken publicly about his work on numerous occasions over the past fifteen years. Fr Pirounakis has perhaps carried the involvement of the parish priest in the day-to-day business of his parishioners to an undesirable extreme, but it is difficult to cavil at a man whose devotion to his parish is such that in 1963 he picked the fifty-three toughest kids in the community and took them on a summer camp with his own children.

It is clear that the in-migrant to the Pirounakis section of Eleusis is not going to feel lost and anonymous among the 7,000 other parishioners for long. He is not going to feel that the parish priest is inaccessible and unconcerned with his problems. He has every chance to participate in parish life, and if he is poor, as in-migrants often are, he may well be receiving food and clothes from the parish. Finding the Church interested in his problems, housing, work conditions, wages, etc., he has an incentive to come to church regularly. On the great feast-days of the Church he may start staying in Eleusis instead of going back to his village of origin. Gradually he will be weaned from the village he has left behind him and become fully integrated into the new urban community he has joined. Having Fr Pirounakis's case before his eyes the in-migrant is unlikely to have much time for Communist agnosticism and denigration of the Church.

So far this discussion has stressed the problems created by mass migration into suburban parishes. What then of the older suburbs with a more fully Athenian population? The parish of St Basil (Saktouri) in Piraeus, the port of Athens, is a fairly typical example of a lower middle-class area, white collar workers, lower grade bureaucrats and skilled workmen. Few of the people in this area are recent in-migrants. The 14,000 parishioners have one first-class, two second-class and one old fourth-class priest (elementary education only). Two priests, one second- and one fourth-class, came in from village parishes during the fifties. The church of St Basil is rarely even half full on an ordinary Sunday morning. The parish priest says his average congregation is about 500 people. In a parish of 14,000 this comes to an ordinary Sunday attendance rate of $3\frac{1}{2}$ per cent. As explained in the previous chapter the Orthodox Church does not make Sunday Mass an obligation under pain of sin, but she does exhort people to take advantage of their day of rest to spend at least a few minutes in church. It must also be borne in mind that people come and go in an Orthodox service so that with a congregation of 500 at say the consecration a total of 700 or 800 people will probably have popped into church between the beginning of Matins at 6 a.m. and the end of Mass at 10 o'clock. Even making allowances for this, the average attendance at St Basil's only goes up to 5 or 6 per cent of the parish. The problem of half-empty churches on ordinary Sundays (on High Feasts all the churches are packed) is a general one in Athens. In a Gallup poll published in the newspaper *Nea* on 21 September 1963 a number of Athenians were asked: "How often do you go to church?" The answers were:

	Per cent
Every Sunday	31
Two or three times a month	32
Once a month	15
On Great Feasts	14
When I have time	3

Most of the 31 per cent of regular church-goers were found to be over forty-five and with incomes of less than £500 per annum. Since few people from the professional and upper middle classes earn less than £500 per year, the Gallup poll indicates that the regular church-goers were on the whole elderly people from the lower middle and working classes.

To return to St Basil's : what does the parish priest there hope to do about his half-empty church? He feels that everything about the parish needs bringing up to date : the priests should look less medieval (doing away with the beard, black cylindrical hat and long trailing sleeves), the church should be air-conditioned, a proper parish hall should be built making the church the focal point in the community, and all the priests should be educated up to university degree standard. This last point is of major importance. As we have seen, only one priest in St Basil's has received an education equivalent to that of an Anglican or Catholic priest. Two of the others have had a secondary school education capped with a hurried two years in a seminary. This means that their educational standard is roughly equivalent to that of an elementary school teacher. The fourth-class priest is virtually uneducated, being able to write only with difficulty. By Western standards a second-class priest is barely adequate to the demands of a town parish and a third- or fourth-class priest is clearly quite inadequate.

The reason for this depressing situation is that out of the 500 theology graduate priests in Greece only 220 are parish priests. The others work as preachers and vicars-general in the provinces or are engaged in the Church's central administration in Athens. Of the 220 theologian parish priests the majority tend to be found in the rich central parishes of the cities, Athens and Salonica, and of the provincial towns, Patras and down. These parishes are in almost exclusively upper middle class areas and are regarded by ambitious unmarried priests as natural stepping-stones to their ultimate goal, the episcopacy. These parish priests with an eye to the future often regard their parish work as something on the way to better things, unlike Fr John of St Stilianos, whose parish is his life. This attitude is accepted among the Greeks—if a man is a reputable theologian priest, and celibate, working in a good central parish, he is felt to be an obvious candidate for the episcopacy: "*páei giá epískopo*". "He's on the way to being a bishop," everyone who knows him says. If he were not, he would have got married before being ordained. It is a source of constant amazement to Orthodox who know them that celibate Catholic priests with years of theology and philosophy behind them should not feel certain that they will sooner or later become bishops.

Financially a central Athenian parish is something well worth having. The theologian priests' £26 per month is handsomely supplemented by the 50 per cent they get of the fees paid for such events as the weddings and christenings that take place in their churches. (The other 50 per cent goes in part to the State, part to the diocese and part to the upkeep of the church.) It is difficult to discover exactly how much a priest in a central parish makes on ceremonies each month, but few of them do less than treble or quadruple their stipends by this means. It is in these central churches that the custom has grown up of having first-, second-, third- and fourth-class ceremonies. The number and rank of the officiating priests, the size of the choir and the number of lights turned on in the church depend on the class of the ceremony, which in turn depends on the price paid. The most expensive you can get is a bishop, a full choir and all the lights in the church turned on. It has become a mark of great social distinction among Athenians to have a "first-class" ceremony in a big central church. This trend unfortunately takes money out of the pockets of the suburban priests and lines the coffers of the central parishes that least need a financial boost.

A similar situation obtains in provincial towns. Two or three central churches attract social climbers who want a bigger wedding or a finer christening than they could have in their own parish church. Few theology graduates are satisfied with less than a good town parish. For instance, there was a young university-trained priest whom I met in a village parish near Volos who expressed indignation at his posting. He gave me to understand that it was unheard of for a man with four years' theology to his credit to be sent to languish in a village. He was expecting a speedy transfer to Volos, the fourth largest town in Greece.

Given that the educational standard of the laity in the central parishes is generally higher than in the suburban ones, one might expect a more intensive approach to instructing people in their faith. On the whole, however, the evangelization, the religious mobilization, of the middle class is carried out, not by the parish priest, but by the monastic brotherhoods such as *Zoi* and *Sotir*, whose work will be dealt with in Chapter 4.

The principal problem that faces the Greek Church on the parish level is the lack of suitable young men wanting to become priests. As we have seen in Chapter 1, the traditional way of filling a parish left vacant by the death of the incumbent priest was for a suitable married and literate peasant of over twenty-five to be chosen by the village elders and sent to the bishop who would normally ordain him after two or three weeks' liturgical training. He was frequently the son of the old priest. Under this system the concept of "vocation" in the meaning of a personal call from God was of little relevance. The priest's role in the village community was an indispensable one; it was an office like that of the village secretary. One had to be honest and God-fearing to become a priest, but hardly any special training was required, and if the priest had land near the village he went on tilling it just like any other villager. So traditionally in the villages the priesthood is a function, a service performed for the good of the community. This attitude to it has been strengthened by the post-war legislation under which priests draw fixed salaries according to their "class", a civil service grading based on the educational standard achieved. While the priesthood in the village tends to be a community office, in a big town parish where the sense of community has been largely lost, the priest's duties have more and more become a job done to get a salary. Since training is now required, the "job" of being a priest has become a profession. A factor that encourages this concept of the priesthood as a profession is the custom that parish priests should be married men. There is much to be said in favour of a country priest being married. The same does not apply to the town priest, whose family is much more of a financial burden to him than is the country priest's. With a bit of land and the £21 a second-class priest gets, plus his "luck money", it is easy to bring up, say, four children in a village. Everything that has to be bought is cheaper and it is less of a strain to "keep up with the Joneses" in housing, consumer goods, education of children, dowries to daughters, etc., in a village than it is in the city. But the legitimate needs of his family drive the city priest to be more grasping and money-minded than his village counterpart.

Only when one realizes that the priesthood is widely regarded as a profession is it possible to understand the obsession of the Holy Synod (council of bishops) with the question of priests' salaries. In October 1962, the 140 priests in the diocese of Volos threatened that they would "go on strike" in a bid for better pay, and early in 1963 the Government increased the salaries of the four classes by rather more than £3 a month. This rise, however, has been largely ineffectual in silencing the grumblings of the Synod about the poverty of the clergy. There *are* exceptional priests who *do* have the idea of a personal vocation to serve God by ministering to his people, but men like Fr George of Ippsilanti (Chapter 1) and Fr John and Fr Pirounakis are few and far between.

Aspirants to the priesthood fall into two categories. Firstly there are the boys from middle-class homes in the towns and some of peasant origin who do the four-year course in the theology faculty of either Athens or Salonica University. There are plenty of theology students following these courses, but very few of them have the slightest intention of becoming priests when they graduate. The profession of lay theology master in a secondary school has a number of substantial advantages over the profession of the priesthood, and especially over becoming a parish priest. The lay theology master generally gets a better salary and he has long holidays; he is not under the thumb of a bishop who may be a trial and he is under no obligation to choose a suitable *pappadiá* (priest's wife) on graduation, as the aspirant parish priest is. (Customarily the parish priest is married, but the marriage must be prior to ordination.) The ironical thing is that while there are only about 220 adequately educated parish priests caring for Greece's eight and a half million Christians, there are so many lay theologians being turned out by the universities that the schools cannot give them all places (see Chapter 6).

Most of the theology students at Athens University live at home or in digs. About 100 of them live in Moni Petraki, a sort of hall of residence, where they receive a loose form of spiritual formation. But even in Moni Petraki there is no concept of spiritual formation similar to that found in Western seminaries—Petraki is more like a religious boarding house with a church on the premises and occasional spiritual direction than a real seminary. The students who do not go to Moni Petraki acquire as much spiritual formation as they are capable of giving themselves. As a result theologian priests are men who have passed the exams at the end of an encyclopaedic theology course, designed to produce competent teachers of the subject, but they have not been consciously trained for the priesthood as such, unless by their own unguided efforts. This is a major weakness in the training of the leaders of the Greek Church, be they educated parish priests, administrators or bishops.

The second category of candidates for the priesthood consists almost exclusively of boys from peasant homes who either go at the age of thirteen to a secondary school-cum-seminary, or do a two-year adult seminary course after having completed their secondary education at a lay school. Both the boys who complete the secondary school-cum-seminary course and those who do the adult course are qualified to become second-class priests. There are ten seminaries and secondary school-cum-seminaries in Greece turning out second-class priests for the ministry in large villages and towns with less than 10,000 inhabitants. It is disquieting to find that more than half of the fifty boys (1964) in the superbly equipped Rizario seminary in Athens were from Epirus, the country's most backward province, and that many of them were the children of village priests. (There is a substantial reduction of fees for the children of priests.) All this suggests that a proportion of these boys are going into the priesthood either because their villages are so poor that the clerical salary is their only hope of anything like a living, or because the priesthood has become a sort of family business. Some of the provincial seminaries take in men who are already priests and give them the training they missed before ordination. Thus a third- or fourth-class *pappás* may rise into the second class and qualify for a better salary. Out of the thirty students in the Volos seminary in 1962 eight were already priests. The students there were all, without exception, peasants.

The seminaries are meant to cater for parishes in large villages and small towns, but what about the growing needs for competent priests in city parishes? Theoretically, city parishes are meant to get university graduates, but in actual fact more and more parishes falling vacant in the Athens–Piraeus area are being filled by ambitious middle-aged country priests. The country priests get themselves to Athens by pulling strings with bishops or, worse still, by pulling political strings in the Ministry of Education and Religion. One typical ploy is for the country priest to get permission from his local bishop to go to Athens to study theology at the university and to take an Athenian parish "on a temporary basis" in order to be able to support his family. Once he gets to Athens the theology course falls into the background and he establishes himself as a regular parish priest. The Bishop of Amphissa has three of these "student priests" in Athens. They have been there so long he described them to me as "pensioner students".

Besides not attempting to cope with the problems of the city parishes, the seminaries have too few pupils even to fill the places vacated by death or migration in the village parishes. Seven hundred communities in Northern Greece are without a parish priest. When a parish falls vacant the bishop tries to fill it temporarily with a monk from a neighbouring monastery, but as the number of monks of working age steadily decreases, this becomes a less and less possible solution.

To sum up : there are ten seminaries in Greece training boys for large village and small town parishes, which leaves out of count the numerous small, inaccessible communities in which many Greek shepherds and peasants still have to live. There are two university theology faculties providing a thin trickle of adequately educated but spiritually unformed priests, less than half of whom go into parish work. The official line is that the two faculties are to supply the two cities and the large towns of Greece with priests. Since this is not happening the vacancies in urban parishes are being filled by inadequate country priests, seized by the general migratory fever that is impelling more and more Greeks towards the towns.

Two reasons may safely be advanced to explain the lack of suitable aspirants to the cloth in the Greek Church today. The first is the unattractiveness of the image of the traditional *pappás*. The image of a semi-illiterate country priest riding a donkey is so current in the towns that it even turns up in advertisements. This sort of image is basically unsympathetic to young people of all classes who have been brought up to think of education as the key to success. Able young Greeks are unlikely to flock to the priesthood until the non-theologian priest has become the shameful exception instead of being the rule. (This is a vicious circle.) The second thing that keeps young men away from the priesthood is the low stipend combined with the prospect of raising a family on it. A priest from a middle-class family, if he is posted to a poor parish, may find himself undertaking to rear his children on a stipend that is nearer to a manual worker's wage than to the salary of a professional person. Very few boys who would make good priests in touch with the modern urban situation are prepared to make the financial and social sacrifices that the priesthood may demand of them and their future families.

ECUMENICAL ATTITUDES IN THE TOWN PARISHES

The "heterodox" of whom both town and country Greeks are most conscious are the Catholics. Those who maintain a fiercely anti-Catholic position regard Anglicans and Protestants in a comparatively kinder light, but even they generally know more about the Catholic Church than about any other Church. This is mainly due to lack of contact with the Anglicans and Protestants at other than bishop level. It will be objected that (i) Britain ruled the seven Ionian islands of Western Greece from 1815 to 1864; (ii) that the World Council of Churches (W.C.C.) has had a large mission in Greece for more than a decade; (iii) that Protestant sects have made numerous conversions in Greek villages. But: (i) The English in the Ionian islands administered, and kept themselves to themselves in the religious as in other fields—as in Cyprus today, they were simply thought of as the *Aggloi* and nobody was much bothered as to what their religion might be about; (ii) the W.C.C.'s mission has played a social and philanthropic part in Greece's recovery from the civil war—though one of its original aims was to promote the ecumenical spirit, most observers are agreed that little ecumenical contact has been made; (iii) the majority of the Orthodox regard the Protestant sects[1] not so much as separated Churches but rather as groups of fanatical heretics of the most unlikely sort, subverting simple peasants with guileful gifts. They do not on the whole connect the proselytizing sects with the hazy ideas they have of the official Anglican and Protestant Churches of Northern Europe and North America. These Churches seem very distant in the popular mind. Not so the Catholic Church. It was the Catholics of the West who in the eleventh century split off from Orthodoxy—Papist crusaders sacked the holy city of Constantinople in 1204 and ruled Greece for nearly a century—the Catholic Doge of Venice held sway over most of the Greek islands for four centuries, indeed Italy only gave back Rhodes after the last war. Greece has a population of 40,000 Catholics in the Aegean Islands, Corfu and in Athens. Consequently when you say "reunion of the Churches" to the average Greek today, he

---

[1] The Evangelicals have been in Greece since 1850 and today have about 30,000 adherents, half of these in Athens. They are split into two Churches, the Greek Evangelical Church and the Free Evangelical Church. There are about 30,000 Jehovah's Witnesses in Greece; apart from a concentration in Athens they seem to be spread in tiny communities all over the country. They started work in 1900. The Seventh Day Adventists and Pentecostalist sects have a following in Greece of rather less than 1 per cent of the population, but what worries the Orthodox hierarchy is that they have made considerable progress since the war. While the Catholics, the only other sizeable non-Orthodox Christian minority, have in a hundred years fallen in numbers from 200,000 to 40,000, the sects have grown from a numerical nothing to 70,000.

immediately thinks of it in terms of the Orthodox and Catholic Churches.

The official Church of Greece has maintained a strongly negative attitude towards even minimal contact with the Catholic Church. The Greek Synod (council of bishops) has blocked nearly all moves towards better relations with Rome. They failed to send observers to any of the sessions of the Vatican Council. They opposed the Pope–Patriarch meeting in the Holy Land in January 1964. In August 1964 the was-to-have-been leader of the Greek delegation to the Third Pan-Orthodox Conference, Bishop Chrysostomos of Argolis (since November 1965 Bishop of Piraeus), spoke of "Abominable ecumenism" in a report prepared for the Archbishop of Athens.[2] The complex feelings of the Greek bishops towards ecumenism will be examined fully in Chapter 5, but officially, at any rate, the Synods have up till now taken a mainly negative stand.

There are several indications that the official anti-Rome policy no longer reflects popular feeling in Greece. The first is the attitude of the press to Rome. Though general coverage of Vatican news is poor, in June 1963 all the newspapers, including those of the extreme left, published long panegyrics on the death of Pope John and favourable forecasts of Pope Paul's reign. Before the Holy Land meeting of the Ecumenical Patriarch and the Pope most Athenian papers came out in favour of it, though their enthusiasm was dampened by the Pope's Bethlehem speech with its invitation to the "Separated Brethren to return to the Fold" (on 6 January 1964). Nearly all the newspapers condemned the Archbishop of Athens' attempt to persuade the other Orthodox Churches to join him in opposing the Patriarch's policy of *rapprochement* with Rome.

[2] The 1963–64 Synod appointed Mgr Chrysostomos of Argolis as head of the Greek delegation to the Third Pan-Orthodox Conference. The 1964–65 Synod, which took over in October 1964, replaced Mgr Chrysostomos as leader of the delegation by Mgr Panteleimon of Salonica, known for his ecumenical views.

Another indication that lay people do not sympathize with the official Church's anti-ecumenical line was a Gallup poll held in Athens in the summer of 1963, in which 62 per cent of those questioned declared themselves to be in favour of the reunion of all the Christian Churches (21 per cent were against reunion and 16 per cent gave no opinion).

A third indication of the gap between the Greek Church's thinking on reunion and popular feeling is the evidence of personal observations by Catholics in Athens. Catholic priests have told me that Orthodox layfolk often ask them if the Churches will ever be reunited and then add, "If only it could be made to happen." I set a class of late teenage students of English a parachute debate—two parachutes for five men in the news: Pope Paul, Mr Khrushchev, Picasso, de Gaulle and Papandreou junior, the then Prime Minister's son. About a third of the class wanted one of the parachutes to go to Pope Paul. When asked to justify their choice they said: "Because he is working for the reunion of the Churches."

One of the most encouraging features of the Greek scene in terms of ecumenism is the surprising amount of knowledge at every level of the population about the differences between Catholicism and Orthodoxy. I have been given more or less well-informed lectures on Catholic "errors" by people as varied as peasants, telephone operators and middle-class businessmen. There are plenty of misconceptions, such as the idea that Catholics believe the pope cannot sin and the failure to understand that he is regarded as infallible only *ex cathedra*: but for all this the amount of knowledge about Catholicism in Greece is astonishing if compared with popular awareness of Orthodoxy in the West. What could a London telephone operator, Anglican or Catholic, tell one about the Orthodox view of the Trinity? This knowledge about Catholic belief and practice has been imparted to the Greeks at school and in catechism classes in a mainly hostile spirit, stressing that the differences between the two Churches are in fact errors on the part of the Catholic Church. The knowledge, none the less, is there, and could well lose its hostile slant as newspaper comment and the atmosphere generally grow gradually more favourable to ecumenism. There is evidence to show that Greek townspeople, especially the better educated, would be more willing to see the Orthodox Church enter into contact with Rome than their parish clergy. A clear example of this was the reaction to a sermon preached in the church of St Panteleimon in Acharnon, a wealthy area in central Athens, on 26 January 1964, three weeks after the Pope–Patriarch Holy Land meeting. The preacher attacked the Pope for wanting to unite the Churches under his single sway. Most of the congregation left the church in the course of the sermon and many people subsequently protested to the local church council that the Pope's words during his Holy Land pilgrimage had not implied at all what the preacher had taken them to mean. Not all the Greek parish clergy are as hostile to contact with the Catholics as this particular preacher, but to a great many Greek town priests it seems that ecumenism is a rather irrelevant pursuit, a wild-goose chase. They have learnt in their theology courses or picked up from the newspapers the points on which the Catholics have strayed from Orthodox teaching, looking at it from their point of view, so until the Pope is willing to abandon at least his major errors what does all this talk about *rapprochement* and even reunion mean? In conversation with many Greek town priests one notices a kind of apathy towards ecumenism based on the conviction that Orthodoxy possesses the full and unadulterated truth in its most perfect form, the dogma of the first seven Ecumenical Councils. One must regretfully admit that this "let them return to the truth if they wish" attitude is not so far removed from the Catholic stand in the days before Pope John's ecumenical bombshell.

In contrast with the widespread apathy and sometimes hostility of the town clergy is the ecumenical enthusiasm of a small group

of Orthodox priests (and lay theologians) who for nearly ten years
now have been holding regular meetings with the Catholics in
Athens to discuss the problems of reunion. The first public result
of this group's activity was a meeting before a packed hall on
13 April 1964, on Catholic–Orthodox reunion, addressed by Fr
Pirounakis (Orthodox) and Fr Stephanou (Catholic). In addition
to his membership of the Orthodox–Catholic discussion group, Fr
Pirounakis used to hold monthly meetings in Eleusis, until his
resignation in June 1964, to discuss ecumenical questions with his
parishioners. His is an intellectual approach to reunion through
exchange of information and discussion of differences. Another
approach is the more practical one of Fr Dimitriadis of Perama, a
parish in the area of the Port of Athens. He feels that the Pope
meeting the Patriarch and eventual theological discussions are, by
themselves, unlikely to produce results—far better that young
people from different Churches should work together on a
common project and thus learn to know and trust each other. He
has had a series of young volunteers from the Lutheran Church of
Sweden doing social work in his desperately poor parish. He says
that the friendliness of these young men, their hard work and their
devoutness when attending Orthodox services have made a lasting
impression on the minds of his parishioners. Fr Dimitriadis main-
tains that this could not have been achieved by mere talk. The idea
that the first step towards reunion should be co-operation in social
and charitable work so that the Orthodox and other Christians get
to know each other is one dear to the heart of the Ecumenical
Patriarch Athenagoras (see Chapter 8). Obviously Fr Pirounakis's
intellectual approach and Fr Dimitriadis's practical work are two
complementary forms of ecumenism.

The ecumenically inclined priests are a tiny minority in Greece
and not more than a dozen or two of these have actively taken part
in ecumenical work, as far as is known. Since there is a growing
majority of lay people in the towns who favour ecumenical con-

act with Rome it becomes pertinent to ask to what extent they will in future let their attitude to ecumenism be influenced by the clergy. Forty-four per cent of the Athenians who replied to the Gallup poll question "What do you think of the clergy?" said that their attitude was not satisfactory. Forty-two per cent of them said the clergy's attitude was satisfactory and 14 per cent gave no opinion. The poll was held in the summer of 1963. In a country like Greece, where the priest is never allowed to remain standing in a bus, where he is the walking symbol of the *Ethnos* (race or nation) and has been so ever since the home policy of the Ottoman Empire forced on him the temporal as well as spiritual leadership of his community, it is a shock to find nearly half those questioned in the Gallup poll were dissatisfied with the clergy. But this dissatisfaction cannot be equated with anti-clericalism in the Western sense, as in, say, Italy or Ireland, where the feeling is against the cassock as such. Western type anti-clericalism is extremely rare in Greece except among people affiliated to the extreme left. Dissatisfaction with the clergy stems from their shortcomings, such as lack of education, their wage-earning rather than vocational attitude to the priesthood, the high charges they levy for ceremonies in central town parishes and the often unseemly manoeuvring of the bishops. But however badly the priest fulfils his duty, he remains to the average Greek the symbol of Greekness as much as of Orthodoxy. Men like Archbishop Makarios in Cyprus reinforce this traditional dual respect for the clergy (see Chapter 7).

Despite the results of the Gallup poll mentioned above it is unlikely that the Greeks will become basically alienated from their clergy as a result of the manifest shortcomings of the latter. What *is* happening, as standards of lay education rise faster than standards of clerical education, is that while the priest retains the emotional respect of the people his power to influence them intellectually is dwindling. The more educated people become the less attention they are likely to pay to fanatical, ill-informed, anti-

ecumenical sermons and articles. There is no doubt that time is
working with the ecumenical spirit in Greece. Thanks to rapidly
rising standards of education, anti-ecumenism based on traditional
and ill-informed fear of Rome will, in the long run, be replaced
among town-dwellers by one of two attitudes : (i) there will be
those who, like Fr Pirounakis, are full-blooded Orthodox but
ardently desire an ecumenical dialogue, and (ii) there will be a
great mass of half a-religious people who in a mild way approve
of the Churches getting together. As the Greeks get progressively
more Europeanized, more and more of them are likely to fall into
the latter category.

3
traditional monasticism

Question: When did you become a monk?

Answer: When I was fifty. I was a soldier from 1912 until 1924 and then I worked in the leather trade.

Q.: Why did you become a monk?

A.: God lit up the way and I came here.

Q: Were you married?

A.: No.

Q.: Are women a bad thing?

A.: Yes.

Q.: But look, I'm married; what should I do?

A.: You should tell your wife you're going to God and then you live together, like brother and sister, not in bed. The best thing would be to tell her to go into a convent and come yourself to be a monk.

Q.: What about children?

A.: Put them in an orphanage.

Q.: But nobody loves them there.

A.: Of course there must be love in an orphanage, like there is in a monastery.

Q.: What was your life like before you became a monk?

A.: In the army I smoked fifteen cigarettes a day, women, drink, went to the theatre—but those were bad things.

Q.: Why is the theatre bad?

A.: Because you see naked women and that's scandalizing.

Q.: But sometimes the actors wear clothes!

A.: Yes, but such light ones you can see what's underneath.

Q.: How do you see the Devil? (meaning what image do you have
of the Devil?)

A.: I've never seen him—only great saints see him. How should I
see him?

Q.: Yes, but what do you think of him?

A.: He makes us like the bad things, women, smoking. . . .

Q.: Why must a monk not smoke?

A.: Because it makes him think of other bad things he could do.

Q.: What do you think of life here?

A.: If you have good will it is easier than life outside—you have a
roof, food, clothing and you go to church often.

This interview with the eighty-year-old porter of the monastery
of Dyonisiou on the western flank of Mount Athos, "the Holy
Mountain", gives a sharp picture of a fairly typical Athonite monk.
The 1,500 monks on the precipitous, richly-wooded peninsula of
Athos in Northern Greece are the main inheritors in the modern
Greek world of the ancient traditions of Orthodox monasticism.
The porter of Dyonisiou is typical in a number of ways. First his
age is typical—very few novices have come to the Holy Mountain
in the post-war years and as a result certain communities are on
the verge of extinction by the death of their last members. In 1913
there were 7,970 monks on Athos (more than half of them Russians). In February 1963 there were only 1,588 left. The porter
monk is typical in being a peasant and in having had little or no
formal education. What he has learnt in his thirty years on Athos
will have been from the liturgy and the hagiographical works that
are read to the monks on the feasts of the various saints. He is
typical, too, in the strength of his faith and the theocentricity of
his thoughts. He was speaking quite seriously in suggesting that I
should shut my wife in a convent, my child in an orphanage, and
become a monk. Even the slackest, shoddiest monks on Athos, of
whom there are a good number, leave one with the impression that

they are strong and total believers. It would be impossible to bear the intensely religious atmosphere of the place if you were not. In this the average Greek monk, especially the Athonite, contrasts strongly with the normal village priest, who, as already explained, sees himself as a village official more than as a man with a mission, called by God. In answer to the question why he became a monk, the old porter answered: "God lit up the way and I came here."

The porter is typical in his over-simplified view of the world outside Athos. To him, as to many others on the Holy Mountain, it is a Sodom and Gomorrah from which they have had the sense, or rather the God-sent enlightenment, to escape. It has been suggested[1] that in the monks' minds there are three hierarchical worlds: (i) God's Kingdom and Hell, as depicted on the walls of the churches, dining halls and cloisters of the monasteries and experienced as very real physical places; (ii) Athos, where the monks strive to lead the "Angelic life" and purge themselves of their evil passions, and (iii) the world outside with its temptations and godless ways.

Finally the porter is typical of a certain number of Athonites in his feeling that being a monk is easier than life outside in the world in the sense that the monk has no money worries and does not have to work to provide himself with a roof, food and clothing. The monks who feel like him about this are usually the ones who like him came to the Mountain late in life, tired of the material struggle to keep alive. But the porter's answer was qualified: "If you have good will" life is easier on Athos—if you are willing to abide by the rule that in some monasteries is very austere, submit to the traditions and accept the manner of thinking of the Athonite community.

There are three stages in the Athonite contemplative life, the "Angelic life". Firstly death to the passions, by retirement from

[1] See Choukas, *Black Angels of Athos* (Stephen Daye Press, Vermont, 1934).

the world and abandonment of pleasure in food, drink, sleep, sex, and so on. This renunciation is achieved by long fasts, all-night offices (*agripnies*) and celibacy to the point that no female animals, apart from cats, are allowed on Athos. The second stage consists in complete cleansing of the thoughts and concentration of the mind on God. This concentration is achieved by the constant repetition aloud or silently of the "Jesus prayer": "Lord Jesus Christ, Son of God, have mercy on me." The Jesus prayer finally gives way to wordless prayer in which the soul silently concentrates on God. The final stage is "deification" (*théosis*) or contemplation of the "Uncreated Light". This is an ideal state that is only granted to a few of the saints to achieve.

The Athonites have evolved five forms of monasticism which to a greater or lesser degree harmonize with the ideal mystical progression outlined above. The first two in historical appearance are perhaps the most compatible with the ascent towards "deification". Athos's first holy men were the hermits who arrived in the eighth and ninth centuries, while the rise of the cenobitic monasteries dates from the founding of the Great Lavra by St Athanasios in the middle of the tenth century. Among the cliffs and ledges of the southern tip of the peninsula there still remain a handful of hermits, their tiny huts accessible only down steps cut in the near vertical rock. The only natural growth there is the prickly pear and if the hermits grow a few of their own vegetables it is because former hermits carried baskets of thin earth down the cliff face from the inhospitable slopes above. There are few of these men left now and over many of the doors I had hoped to knock on there was a withered branch, signifying the recent death of the occupant.

Of the twenty self-governing monasteries on Athos eleven are cenobitic, which means that the monks worship and eat together. The cenobitic monasteries are the strictest on the mountain—they keep each of the fifty or so all-night vigils in the year, which means that in some cases the monks spend fifteen hours on end in church

On the whole the most seriously-minded novices gravitate towards the cenobitic monasteries. The cenobitic monasteries are ruled by an abbot elected for life who is advised by an annually elected committee. It is the abbot, however, who has effective spiritual and administrative power—he is often a theologian which gives him a high degree of prestige among the less educated monks, in spite of the Athonite's proclaimed contempt for learning.

The third Athonite way of life is to be found in the idiorhythmic monasteries of which there are nine. The idiorhythmic system grew up in the fifteenth century and has troubled the consciences of the stricter monks ever since. In these nine monasteries each monk has his own room or flat in which he cooks and eats his meals, reads, works and lives. While in the cenobitic monastery attendance at divine office is binding on all, in the idiorhythmic houses only those monks officiating that week are bound to be in church. Each monk is paid for his particular *diakonía* or service and with this money he buys most of his own food, clothes, shoes, and so on. The idiorhythmic monasteries keep only a few of the all-night vigils and as each man cooks for himself the rigid observance of the fasts is a matter of individual conscience. Since the idiorhythmic life is easier than the cenobitic, the novices it attracts are often less spiritually and certainly less ascetically inclined people. There are many more monks in the idiorhythmic than in cenobitic houses who have come simply to escape the material worries of the outside world. The idiorhythmic house is ruled oligarchically by the *proestámenoi*, superiors, who annually elect a committee of three of their number which is responsible for the affairs of the monastery. About 10 per cent of the monks in the monastery are superiors and when a superior dies his peers elect another monk to fill the vacant place. The title of abbot is honorific and the monk who holds it wields no effective power.

Though the twenty monasteries have lost the vast estates they once owned all over the Balkans (including Greece), most of them

C

are still comparatively well off. Many monasteries own real estate
in the booming towns of Salonica and Athens and even if they did
not they could easily subsist from the sale of the peninsula's timber.
Many of the telegraph poles in Greece are Athonite. As a result of
the money the monasteries earn in this way, few of their inmates
are ever involved in strenuous physical work. The felling of timber
and the cultivation of the land is done by hired labourers. The
exception to this is the guest-master who in the summer may
find himself cooking for anything up to seventy pilgrims and
tourists.

Work, however, is an integral part of the monk's day in the last
two Athonite forms of monasticism. The monks who are neither
hermits nor members of cenobitic or idiorhythmic monasteries live
in a *kellí* or a *skíti*. A *kellí* consists of an elder and two or three
younger monks under him leading a communal life in a self-
contained cottage. A *skíti* is a scattered village of such cottages
each house with its elder but the whole community sharing the
same church and recognizing the authority of an elected prior. (All
kelliá and *skítes* ultimately depend on a mother monastery, one
of the twenty.) These monks make a living from what they grow
or manufacture for export outside Athos. The craftsmen monks
include icon-painters, wood-carvers, rosary-makers and gold-
smiths. To a Western way of thinking their life is more balanced
than that of the hermit or the strict cenobitic monk since they
divide their time between the divine office and productive work
leading a life of Benedictine-like measure.

While novices coming to the monasteries are usually adults the
kellí novices are recruited much younger. Frequently they are
relatives of the monks and go to Athos as young as twelve or
thirteen years old. In an all-male community the introduction of
boys of this age must give rise to some homosexuality—it is clearly
impossible to gauge how much there actually is. Despite this
danger the *kellí* novices are formed on Athos; they are virtually

brought up there. Not knowing the world outside and having been instilled with an antipathy towards it, they have no desire to leave. By contrast the dwindling number of monastery novices mostly come older and often leave after the first few weeks or at most months. The *kelliá* seem to be the only communities on Athos which maintain a normal balance between youth and age. About one-fifth of the Athonites live in these little family-like communities.

Other than in the *kelliá* communities the visitor to Athos is confronted with scenes of pathetic decline. The huge echoing quadrangles and cloisters of the twenty main monasteries leave one with the impression of Oxford colleges during the winter vacation, with one or two hurrying figures crossing the flagstones, and over all a sense of immense abandonment. This feeling is accentuated on Athos by the physical dilapidation of certain monasteries. The most startling evidence of decline is to be seen in the Russian monastery of St Panteleimon. Built by the Tzarist Russians to house 1,500 monks, and before the First World War it did, St Panteleimon is an enormous nineteenth-century palace with four large churches and innumerable outhouses. In 1963, thirty monks lived in one of the great six-storey buildings on the main quadrangle. The youngest monk was then sixty-four. Everywhere outside this main square one sees broken windows, doors off their hinges and roofs beginning to fall in. At night the only sounds are the shrieking of cats and the slow shuffle of an old monk's slippered feet along one of the corridors or balconies. I was shown the names of the three monks who had died in the first three weeks of February 1963 chalked up on a black slate outside the abbot's door. The last novice entered St Panteleimon in 1942 and despite various noises made by both the Russian Orthodox Church and the State about sending a fresh batch of monks from Russia, nothing has happened at the time of writing (spring 1965). The decline of the Russian houses on Athos has been much more pre-

cipitate than that of the Greek monasteries, due to the closing of
the Russian frontiers in 1917 and to the considerable difficulties put
in the way of would-be Russian novices. The abbot of St Panteleimon even alleged that the monastery's correspondence is
censored by the local Greek authorities. The Greek Civil Governor
of Athos told me that this was not the case, but the denials of a
cornered official are sometimes tantamount to a confirmation. The
Greek Government's main fear is that Russian novices might be
spies. This fear, added to a general antipathy towards her northern
Slav neighbours, accounts for Greece's exclusionary policy.

Though the plight of St Panteleimon is an extreme case, most
Greek monasteries are on the way to being in the same position.
The average monastery counts about thirty-five monks while having room for three or four hundred. The Holy Mountain has often
faced and weathered the threat of extinction, but in the past the
threat has always been external: one thinks of the massacres by
Catalan mercenaries (1307–9), the Sultan's crushing taxation, the
Turkish military occupation during the 1821 War of Independence
when most of the monks fled from Athos, and so on. The present
crisis on Athos goes deeper since for the first time in 1,000 years
the Eastern monastic ideal seems to be losing its grip on the youth
of Orthodox Greece.

To explain adequately how this has come about it is necessary to
examine what the Athonite life offers a young Greek of today. As
we have seen, he is offered a life free from financial responsibility
and removed from family difficulties and frictions. On Athos his
aesthetic sense is satisfied by the beauty of the divine office, the
frescoes in the church and the refectory and above all by the
breath-taking natural beauty of the peninsula itself, often called
the Garden of the *Panagía* (our Lady's Garden). His imagination
is filled by the oral traditions of Athos, rich in legends of saints
and stories of miracles. Even the more knowing and worldly
monks I met accept the stories of local miracles as historically true.

A well-educated eighteen-year-old novice, living in a dream-world of Athonite legend, told me of the monk who did not believe that the icon of the Virgin at Iviron had shed real blood when stabbed by a heathen pirate: ". . . the unbelieving monk stole down to the church one night and touched the icon to see if the blood had not been painted on—the icon started bleeding and the terrified monk went back to his cell and died of fright". Above all, life on the Holy Mountain offers the religiously inclined young man the opportunity of doing more to save his soul than he would be likely to do "in the world".

There are, however, many negative factors working against a young Greek wanting to become an Athonite monk. The first and perhaps most important is the ultra-conservatism that reigns on Athos. The conservative spirit has been so predominant that Athonite life is still in many respects a faithful replica of life in the late Byzantine Empire. Time is measured according to the twelve-hour Byzantine clock so that, for example, 7 a.m. is the first hour and 3 p.m. the ninth hour. Athos has retained the Julian calendar, thirteen days behind the Gregorian or Western calendar, although this was dropped in Greece in 1924. Most of the monasteries are connected by paths that will not take a wheeled vehicle and there is no road into Athos from Greece—you have to go along the rocky coast by boat. The monks themselves are fanatically conservative and refuse to alter the slightest thing about their way of life or worship. If something is laid down by tradition it cannot be changed, however needful and logical an alteration may be. Since female animals are traditionally barred from Athos, the stricter of the icon painters who need yolk to mix with their colours, import their eggs from Greece in order to avoid the sin of keeping hens! A young Greek thinking of going to the Holy Mountain knows that he will be under the spiritual direction of an elderly monk who will almost certainly be a fanatical traditionalist down to the last insignificant detail.

The second main factor working against the maturation of a monastic vocation is the general contempt in which education is held on the Mountain. Some monks go as far as to stigmatize book-learning as a temptation to pride sent by the Devil. Even the few educated monks (there are two or three theologians in each monastery) say that learning is inessential to the mystical way the monk should attempt to follow—the "Angelic life". So the layer of dust on the books and manuscripts in the great libraries of Athos lies almost undisturbed except for occasional visits by outside academics. Formerly Athos was a centre of learning and during the Turkish occupation of Greece it became a seminary for bishops, owing to the comparative autonomy the Sultan had granted the monks. The tradition that Athos should supply Greece with bishops persisted after the 1821 revolution, though today it is on the wane. In 1965 at least six of Greece's fifty-five or so bishops were ex-Athonites. The elevation of ignorance and lack of education into a virtue by the majority of the monks of Athos is totally antipathetic to the average young Greek, who, on the contrary, sees education as the key to every sort of improvement in his life. Proof of this is that only one in six of the pupils of the Athonite theological seminary, which was created to feed theologians to the monasteries, actually become monks when they have finished their six-year course.

Apart from the monks' conservatism and obscurantism a host of other factors tend to devalue the monastic ideal in the eyes of modern young Greeks. Many monks are dirty and unkempt at a time when cleanliness is a motto you see pinned up on the walls of all primary schools. They have the reputation of being immoral, since naturally the popular newspapers seize on any whiff of scandal while passing over the many hundreds of cases of monks who lead ordinary lives. Nearer to the time of the Revolution (1821) there was a nationalistic, patriotic flavour to joining a monastery, since the monasteries had helped to keep alive Greek letters during the Turkish occupation. With the passage of time people have become less emotionally aware of the link between the monasteries and the *Ethnos* (race or nation).

Despite the faith of the monks of Athos that God will not allow monasticism to wither away in the Garden of the *Panagía*, it is difficult to have much realistic hope in the future. There is absolutely nothing to indicate that more young men will join the monasteries. On the contrary, the trickle of vocations will probably dwindle yet further. Given the beauty of the place, the historical interest of the buildings and the value of the books and frescoes in the monasteries, there is likely to be more and more pressure on the Government to turn the peninsula into a cultural and tourist centre. As long as there are monks in the monasteries they will bitterly and probably successfully oppose such a move, but once they are gone . . . ? To my mind the only realistic hope for the continuance of the monastic life on Athos lies in the *kelliá*, whose monks could continue their life of prayer and work even if the twenty monasteries were to turn into gaping grounds for tourists.

Though the heart of what remains of the old mystical monasticism is to be found on the slopes of Mount Athos, Greece as a whole is a land studded with monasteries. On an inaccessible shoulder or hilltop, on a ledge at the base of a cliff, clinging to the sides of a ravine, you will find monasteries all over the country (excluding Eastern Macedonia and Thrace). No clearer indication of the Greek monk's ascetic view of the way of salvation can be given than his habit of always discovering the most barren and inhospitable site in the area for the foundation of a new religious house, sites which contrast strikingly with the rich farm lands surrounding most medieval English monasteries.

The monks of Greece, as opposed to the Athonites, live either in cenobitic or idiorhythmic monasteries—it is extremely rare to find hermits or *kelliá*, and *skítes* do not exist in Greece outside

Athos. Though their monasticism is fundamentally exactly the same as that of the Athonites, the monks of Greece live in a different situation and have to face somewhat different problems.

While Athos is an internally self-governing state ruled by the Holy Community (a committee of twenty representatives from the twenty monasteries), the monasteries of Greece come directly under the jurisdiction of the local bishop. This usually means that in all important matters the abbot acts as lieutenant to the bishop and not as a responsible leader. If the bishop is an energetic and holy man his overseeing brief ensures discipline in the monastery. If he is not energetic and never visits some remote monastery, then the cat's away and the mice will play. This unfortunately is the case in many of Greece's monasteries.

While the monastic community on Athos has as its sole aim the sanctification of its members, the Greek monastery also plays a part in the religious life of the area in which it is situated. Traditionally the monastery is the religious centre for the nearby villages —the peasants go there to confession, to baptize their children, to pray to the saint of the monastery and to reverence his relics. Since a village may be many hours' walk from the monastery the monks have evolved a tradition of great hospitality. They provide the pilgrim with food and a bed. When the monastery served only the surrounding villages this hospitality was quite compatible with carrying on a normal religious life. Since the war, however, things have changed—as more and more roads have been built the better-known monasteries have turned into national and even international tourist centres, as well as being places of pilgrimage. Perhaps the worst hit is Osios Loukas, off the road from Athens to Delphi, which in 1963 was visited by 300,000 people. The State has taken over the church and a hotel has been built beside the monastery so that the twelve resident monks do not have to spend their time looking after the tourists, but for all that, as far as retirement from the world is concerned, they might as well be living in the centre of Athens. Osios Loukas is an extreme example and the bulk of its visitors are foreigners.

The tourism most dangerous to the survival of the monasteries as religious houses is the habit growing up among middle-class Athenians of going on week-end charabanc excursions to places of interest. The attraction the monasteries hold for them is mainly historical and scenic—such excursions can in no way be described as pilgrimages. An example of a monastery beset by Greek middle-class tourists is Megaspilaion in the Peloponnese where during 1963 the twenty-two monks coped with 200,000 Greek visitors and 8,000 foreigners. In the summer they have as many as six or seven coachloads of people each evening wanting to sleep in the monastery. Several of the monks are too old to do anything active and the rest are obliged to live more as hotel-cum-museum keepers than as monks.

Perhaps the most striking difference between the monasteries of Athos and those of Greece is that the theocentric atmosphere of the Holy Mountain is often absent even in the more secluded Greek houses. One of the main reasons for this is that many Greek monasteries no longer constitute numerically viable communities. While the average Athos house still has thirty to forty monks, Greek monasteries described as being "in action" may have as few as two or three octogenarian monks, remnants of past communities. An example of this is the great hill-top monastery of Varnachova, which in 1964 had only four monks in residence. The depletion of the monastic communities is taken a step further when the local bishop finds himself short of parish priests and is forced to fill vacant parishes with priest-monks. Nearly all Greek monastic communities have been depleted by the needs of the surrounding parishes. Such few young Greeks as feel the pull of the traditional monastic life, on the whole prefer to become Athonites than join an obviously dying local religious community.

A glance at the ten-year-old ecclesiastical map of Greece shows that even in the mid-fifties there were many more abandoned monasteries than inhabited ones. In other words the blight affecting male monasticism has progressed further in Greece than on Athos. What happens to a monastery when the last monk dies? In practice six answers have been found : (i) If the church and buildings are of sufficient interest historically and artistically they may be taken over by the State Archaeological Service and turned into museums (e.g. Daphni); (ii) here and there a monastery has been turned into a hotel, but this solution has now been ruled out by the Holy Synod (e.g. Trikeri, near Volos); (iii) the bishop may decide to use the monastic buildings to house a diocesan charitable foundation, an old people's home or an orphanage (e.g. Arta); (iv) the local bishop may revive the monastery by importing new monks from outside his diocese (e.g. the diocese of Trikkis and Stagon); (v) the abandoned buildings may be used to house a group of nuns (e.g. in the diocese of Attica), and (vi) the deserted monastery may be left to crumble, a respected memorial, which is what happens in the majority of cases.

A major attempt to revive dying monasteries by the importation of new young monks is to the credit of Bishop Dyonisios of Trikkis and Stagon in Central Greece. When he arrived in his see in 1959 he found the crag-top monasteries of Meteora inhabited by remnant communities, monks whom he regarded as slack and work-shy. His first action was to remove them to a monastery at the other end of the diocese from Meteora. Having modernized the living facilities in two of the main monasteries he installed a nucleus of university graduates in both houses, plus a complement of less educated monks. He conceives monasticism as having an evangelical mission and the educated monks were given a Volkswagen to allow them to go down from their eagle's nests each day to take catechism classes and to preach in the towns of the diocese. The experiment worked for a year and then in 1962 the nucleus in Barlaam decided to go back to Athens. The main reasons for this decision were the pressure of tourism, which rendered a truly religious life difficult, and a difference of opinion between the leader of the group and Bishop Dyonisios as to how much say the latter should have in the running of the monastery. In 1965, after the departure of the graduates, Barlaam had seven monks, four of whom had been to secondary school. In the second monastery, Metamorphoseos, the graduate nucleus did not leave, but it has proved impossible to harmonize the demands of a preaching apostolate with the traditional monastic life. One of the three educated monks resides in the monastery and instructs the novices while the other two live down in the town of Trikkala, catechizing and preaching. They pay as frequent visits as they can to the monastery but they can hardly be called monks, at any rate not in the traditional sense. One of the real innovations in the Meteora monasteries is the restriction of visiting hours and the realization that a monastery visited by 5,000 tourists a day cannot offer the old style hospitality that used to be extended to pilgrims. No visitor may eat or sleep in the monasteries without the bishop's express permission. However, to preserve the principle of hospitality each visitor is offered a Turkish delight and a glass of water. There might be more hope for male monasticism in Greece if more of the bishops were as energetic as Mgr Dyonisios.

One of the most surprising things about the monastic scene in Greece is the mushrooming of little communities of nuns that has been going on especially since World War II. Time and time again one finds that a woman has gathered a little like-minded band round her and got permission from the local bishop to start a convent. In the diocese of Attica, for instance, there are seven communities of nuns, six of which have been brought into being since 1945. They are all housed in abandoned monasteries. In contrast to the monks, who tend to live like Western choir monks minus their intellectual work, these nuns work all the hours of the day they are not attending divine office. The occupations of the nuns in the diocese of Attica include painting icons, weaving, knitting socks, and making vestments. Unlike most of the monasteries, these new convents have no land or real estate to live off and so they depend entirely on their own earnings and the offerings of local people. Increasingly these little convents are being founded with a social aim. Of the two main convents in the diocese of Trikkis one runs a three-year handicraft course for peasant girls who have finished elementary school, and the other is about to open an orphanage with its own elementary school attached.

In some cases a new community of nuns has not only taken over an abandoned monastery but reinstated it as the spiritual centre of the area round. The diocese of Thebes and Levadeia gives a typical idea of the decline of male and the rise of female monasticism. At the time of writing (spring 1965) four monasteries have been completely abandoned and four are hanging on by a thread with complements of respectively twelve, four, four and two monks. In 1960 a tiny group of nuns took over the abandoned Evangelistria monastery, propped up wobbly walls, re-roofed rafters that had been bare to the sky and turned the place once again into a religious house. Today there are eight nuns with a prospect of four young novices coming in the near future. In 1964 the nuns added a whole new wing with money provided by the surrounding villages. The convent has become a place of pilgrimage and frequently local people prefer to go to confession and christen their children there than in their own villages. While an atmosphere of hopelessness reigns among the ageing monks of Boeotia, the nuns of the Evangelistria convent are young and full of life. There is a feeling of prayerfulness and discipline in this and many of the other new convents that one looks for in vain in the monasteries.

In most cases the idea of going into a convent occurs to girls who attend catechism class and the foundresses normally recruit their first novices either from their own circle of relations and friends or from the catechism classes. Sometimes the first nucleus is formed by a priest who influences his most suitable catechism pupils towards the monastic life. The new convents attract novices from the towns as well as from the villages and the girls who come are by no means the most uneducated in the community. Often they have had a complete or partial secondary education.

It is impossible to find a fully satisfactory answer as to why girls go into convents at a time when none of their brothers want to become monks. However, two things obviously influence the situation. Firstly parents are much more opposed to a son entering a declining monastery than to a daughter becoming a nun in an up-and-coming convent. The image of the hard-working, spiritual nun contrasts with the picture many Greek people have of a dirty, unkempt, uneducated, lax monk. Secondly, if a poor family has many daughters there is unlikely to be enough money for them all to be given dowries good enough to catch a husband. A girl knowing of a good convent and facing the prospect of becoming an old maid with no means of support may quite naturally find her thoughts turning towards the monastic life.

THE MONKS AND ECUMENISM

As far as attitudes to ecumenism are concerned the monks of Athos and the rest of Greece can be taken together. (As a rule nuns do not read the newspapers and are uninformed about ecumenical questions.) As we have seen, the monks are arch-conservatives and one of their traditions is suspicion and dislike of the Catholic Church and especially of the Papacy. When confronted in the newspapers and on the radio with news about steps towards *rapprochement* between the Orthodox and Catholic Churches the monks react in two main ways. The most fanatical accuse the Orthodox leaders involved of "betraying Orthodoxy", of selling the faith down the river. The more level-headed monks admit that saying "good-day" to separated Christians is allowable but make it quite clear that the presupposition of any sort of reunion is that Rome should abandon her many errors, which they feel to be a highly unlikely contingency. An icon painter on Athos told me this story which aptly illustrates the monks' view of the East-West schism and the Reformation: "One of our pappades and a Franco-Romeo pappás were travelling to Athos in a fishing boat. The Catholic talked and talked and when he had finished the people round asked the Orthodox to answer him. Our pappás took a piece of paper from his pocket, tore it down the middle and put one half back into his pocket—Orthodoxy. The other half he tore into small pieces and let them flutter over the stern of the boat, saying: 'That is what happened to the Romans when they left us'."

Most monks, even the most uneducated ones, are informed about ecumenical questions and the Catholic Church, though often in an addle-pated way. What is lacking with many monks is a sense of proportion in judging the relative importance of the things separating the two Churches. A monk will attack the Catholic conception of the Papacy in the same breath as he inveighs against the iniquity of priests being clean-shaven (all Orthodox priests and monks are obliged to wear beards). The lack of balance in the monks' view of Rome is a result of two things: (i) the fiercely anti-Catholic tradition of Eastern monasticism (it was the fifteenth-century monks of Constantinople who roused the people of the Byzantine capital against the shaky Catholic–Orthodox reunion negotiated at the Council of Florence); (ii) the fact that large numbers of intellectually untrained monks have the leisure to gather up scraps of information about the Catholic Church, chew them over in a hostile environment and arrive at invalid or over-simplified conclusions. This is an example of a particularly un-balanced and garbled tirade I was subjected to on Athos in 1963: "We would be ready to shoot the Ecumenical Patriarch if he sent observers to the Vatican Council; our Church forbids us to set foot in Catholic churches. The Catholics don't believe in Mary's virginity. None of the bodies of your saints has remained intact, not since the schism. Western priests shave their beards off and the Seventh Council vowed anathema on shaven priests. I wouldn't kiss the hand of a priest who shaved his beard. Why does the Pope wear rings? Where does that come in the Gospels? The Prophets said, 'Make ye no idols', so if we were reunited the Catholics would have to get rid of their statues."

The educated theologian monks do not talk the above sort of nonsense, but few of those I met can envisage Orthodoxy giving even an inch of ground. Fr Athanasios, the learned librarian of Iviron (Athos), who was formerly Orthodox chaplain in Naples, told me that Orthodoxy had all the complaints against Rome and that Rome could find nothing with which to reproach Orthodoxy. Fr Athanasios would not even agree that fashions change : "Shaving is a complete emasculation, and for the first priest, the Pope, to shave off his beard is quite unthinkable."

Very occasionally and usually outside Athos, one meets a monk who could be called ecumenically minded in the sense that he regards the matters dividing the two Churches as differences and not necessarily errors on the part of either Church. One such monk told me that we should not speak of one Church breaking off from the other at the time of the schism, but of the one Church dividing into two separate streams, the Orthodox and the Catholic. He was delighted when I told him of the renaissance of patristic studies in the West as he felt this would help Catholics and Protestants to understand the Orthodox position, based on the dogmatic teaching of the first Seven Councils and the writings of the Fathers. A clear indication of the anti-ecumenical atmosphere in which this liberal-minded monk lives is that at the end of our very frank discussion he made me promise that I would not reveal his name, for fear of what his fellow monks and the local bishop might think.

With a very few individual exceptions, the monks are emotionally the most anti-ecumenically disposed group in Greek society. Their influence on the thinking of educated lay people is negligible and likely to decrease still further with the continued decline of the monasteries. However, the influence they still have on the uneducated laity is not to be disregarded. Apart from the 1,500 or so monks on Athos there are 800 ex-Athonites in Greece working as chaplains, parish priests and, in the case of theologian monks, as preachers and confessors. They help to keep alive the latent suspicion of Rome that is a kind of Greek birthright.

4

the new monasticism and the
lay apostolate

THE PRINCIPAL aim of traditional Eastern monasticism is that each
monk should abandon the world, live the mystical progression
outlined in Chapter 3 and thus attain his own personal salvation.
This tradition grew out of the needs of the fourth-century Christians in the Near East whose faith, after generations of persecution,
had suddenly become the religion of the whole Empire, the estab-
lishment ideology. The fourth-century saints who took to the
desert and who are the founders of the tradition of Eastern monasticism, felt the need to seek God personally, in solitude, away from
the flabby, too easily accepted, institutionalized Christianity of the
great cities, like Alexandria.

In a parallel way the new monasticism of the brotherhoods of
theologians was born from the needs of nineteenth- and early
twentieth-century Christianity in Greece. The middle of the last
century saw Orthodoxy in Greece drifting in a state of rudderless
exhaustion. The clergy were almost all illiterate, the episcopate was
reduced to four aged bishops, there was no one to preach the
essentials of the faith to the people, and the sacraments of confession and communion had fallen into almost complete disuse.
The handful of inspired men, who in the fourth century would
probably have fled to the desert to lead a life of contemplation, in
the second half of the nineteenth century decided that their main
task was to go out into the squares of the main towns of Greece
and remind their nominally Christian countrymen what the faith
was about. Some of these itinerant preachers were laymen, some

priests and some monks; the priests among them would spend long
hours in the confessional. Though loosely associated by their
common mission these men worked separately and unco-ordin-
atedly. It was not until 1907 that one of them, Fr Eusebius
Matthopoulos, convinced that the re-evangelization of Greece could
never be achieved by isolated preachers working on their own,
gathered round him a group of young theologians, mainly laymen,
who were to form the nucleus of the Brotherhood of *Zoi* (life).

Today *Zoi* has 100 members (the Brotherhood)—nearly all are
theologians and about one-fifth of these are priests. Non-clerical
theologian brothers wear ordinary lay clothes. On entering the
community the *Zoi* brother takes solemn promises (not vows) of
poverty, chastity and obedience. In principle the brothers live a
cenobitic life in their central house in Athens, but for many of
them this is not possible in practice, since one third are stationed
permanently away in the provinces, and even those resident in
Athens often have to be absent on preaching tours. Once a year
all the brothers gather for a month-long retreat during which the
progress of their work is reviewed and future policy is formed. The
Brotherhood is ruled by a superior, and a council elected by the
brothers. The system is basically parliamentarian. Given the pressure of their practical work it is impossible for the brothers to
attend long hours of divine office as the traditional monks do. This
is replaced by half an hour of communal prayer at the beginning
and end of each day.

What *Zoi* has set out to do is no less than to reform the Greeks'
attitude to Christianity. The basis of the Brotherhood's message
is repentance, followed by a personal and practical commitment to
living one's religion as an individual. Hence the great emphasis
they place on the sacraments of confession and communion. One
of the main features of the *Zoi* liturgical reform is the stress on the
necessity of frequent communion. Habitually the Orthodox have
gone to communion only on the four great feastdays in the year,

and until recently it was felt that only a very holy person might dare to communicate more frequently. *Zoi* sets out to change this mentality and in the cities has partially succeeded. In many Athenian parishes one sees twenty or thirty people going to communion every Sunday in the year.

As a corollary of the need to repent, the *Zoi* brothers see strict personal morality as a necessary basis to the Christian life. It is not enough to go to church regularly—a Christian must avoid sin and the excesses of the modern world. Sometimes this stress on the moral dangers of the modern world reaches a puritanical pitch as in this excerpt from an article on "The Twist: a mortal danger" in the *Zoi* magazine (21 February 1963): "So each new dance we are presented with acts as a bulldozer destroying and levelling the holy places of the soul. The dance takes the form of an iconoclastic craze which leaves nothing standing. Awareness of goodness, honour, decency and dignity is trampled under foot by the dance. Snobbery and a mania for foreign things work together in close liaison for the destruction of every moral and civilized value." This, however, is an extreme example and on the whole *Zoi's* moral teaching stays within the bounds of reason.

The constant effort of the Brotherhood in its preaching, catechism classes, publications and radio broadcasts is to rouse the people from a merely formal and outward Christianity to an active, personally committed faith. On 31 January 1963, the *Zoi* magazine had an article entitled "Love Ye War": "What kind of war does the Christian wage? He takes up his spiritual weapons and begins the struggle by attacking the evil in his own soul. He decides to struggle for deliverance from the passions of anger, drunkenness, stealing, lying and immorality. As long as he fights under the flag of the risen Christ he is sure to win. Many people in our day have as their ideal an easy, flabby life without either effort or trouble. Ours is an age in which struggle is continually being rejected. This is why we Christians in this time of peace should love war.

We must fight more systematically to win the battle of love and justice. Without struggle life has no meaning."

Zoi does not restrict itself to urging the faithful to live their Christianity more fully—it is actively concerned to reform the Orthodox Church's practice and remove abuses that keep people away from church. In an article entitled "Liturgical viewpoints" in the *Zoi* magazine (17 January 1963) the following points are made : [1] 8,000 priests have the privilege of saying Mass each week for eight million Greeks. They must realize and feel the wonder of this. But piety is not enough. A basic question is the length of the service. This is laid down by the bishops and must be put into practice by the priests. Prolongation of the service tires people, makes them complain and harms their spirituality. It drives people away from church. The church itself should always be a place of order, decency and civilization. There must be quiet and cleanliness. There must be seating arrangements and heating for the winter months. In all other fields, military, educational, economic, there is supervision. There are special supervisors. This is lacking in the religious field. Each priest decides, reduces or corrects as he thinks fit. Matters have reached a point of ridicule and impiety. Inspection is the bishop's duty—if he cannot inspect personally he should delegate to the vicar-general or to the preacher priests. . . . At any rate a stop must be put to this immunity, irresponsibility and "that's the way I like it" attitude.

Apart from wanting to reduce the length of the eucharistic service by cutting out matins (which normally precedes the Mass itself) and by reducing the repetition in the chanting, *Zoi* also insists that there should be more participation by the congregation in the service. To this end it has introduced the singing of hymns by the congregation, where formerly the only voices heard were those of the celebrants, the cantors and the choir.

It was clear from the inception of the *Zoi* Brotherhood that a

[1] What follows is a résumé of the article.

small group of men, however hard-working, would never be able to evangelize directly the whole of Greece by the spoken word. Four years after the founding of the Brotherhood, in 1911, they began bringing out the *Zoi* magazine, which from the beginning had the practical slant illustrated by the already-quoted extracts from it. *Zoi* now sells 120,000 copies each week, a figure well ahead of any other Greek magazine for adults, religious or secular. It is distributed by post and reaches subscribers even in far-away villages on the Albanian border.

The Brotherhood was determined to encourage study of the Bible among lay people and to this end has started hundreds of Bible study groups. The first step was to translate the Gospels and Epistles from archaic Greek into the modern idiom. This was done in the 1930s and since then the New Testament translation has sold 680,000 copies in thirty-two editions. A statistical proof of *Zoi's* success in promoting Bible study is that over a five-year period a commentary on the New Testament sold 80,000 copies.

The massive success of the movement started by the monks of the *Zoi* Brotherhood is not due to their admirable aims and the disciplined devoutness of their own lives alone. A large part of this success must be attributed to the foresight with which they have involved the middle classes in active participation in the home missionary movement. There are today twelve associations affiliated to *Zoi* each of which aims to evangelize one particular section of the population. Each association has a *Zoi* brother as its director and follows the line laid down by the *Zoi* governing council. So wide is the field covered directly by the Brotherhood, by *Eusebia*, the corresponding women's monastic community, and by the twelve lay organizations that most occupational and age groups in the population are, at least in theory, catered for. The primary-school child can attend Sunday catechism class given by a member of the Students' Association and can read the *Zoi* children's magazine (circulation 160,000) compiled by the *Eusebia* sisters. If he lives in a village, the primary-school child can go to catechism class given by a member of the *Zoi* Association of Teachers. The secondary-school child can continue learning about his faith in the senior catechism classes normally taught by members either of the Students' Association or of the Professional People's Association. If he is particularly religiously inclined the secondary-school child may be chosen to join one of the seminar groups whose members are given a special formation with a view to becoming leaders in the future. They are taken on special holiday camps in the summer. The University student may decide to lead a strictly disciplined life in a *Zoi* run hostel and he may also join the Students' Association mentioned above. When he has taken his degree he can join the Professional People's Association, which produces a magazine of its own, organizes lectures, discussion groups and Bible study meetings. The primary-school teacher, lost in some mountain village, may draw consolation from belonging to the Teachers' Association. Parents have the Parents' Association to join and young workers can become members of the Association of Working Youth.

Each association has its own magazine geared to the age, intellectual capacity and interests of its members. *Aktines*, for instance, the Professional People's journal, is one of the foremost intellectual publications on the Greek magazine market. It carries articles on subjects of general scholarly interest as well as on specifically religious matters. The Teachers' Association has produced twenty books solely devoted to pedagogical problems. In each Greek town where there is a resident *Zoi* brother some of the associations have branches. In Salonica, for instance, all the *Zoi* affiliated associations have branches. It is through the associations that the 100 *Zoi* brothers have been able to broadcast and put into practice on a national scale their ideas on the spiritual, moral and organizational renovation of religious life in Greece.

Chapters 1 and 2 will have made clear the inadequacy of the

average parish priest as a pastor. It is clearly the parish priest who should be organizing catechism classes, doing social work in his area, organizing visits to the sick, running summer camps, etc., not an outside organization like the *Zoi* movement. What has happened in many town parishes both in Athens and elsewhere is that the *Zoi* movement has stepped in and filled the spiritual and organizational vacuum left by an inadequate parish priest. In the provinces this often causes friction with the diocesan authorities. There are quite a number of bishops who feel uncomfortable when a *Zoi* brother comes to reside in their diocesan town. Bishop Seraphim of Ioannina told me the brothers were "merchants" rather than monks (because they run religious bookshops). When *Zoi* sent a new man to Ioannina in 1960 this same bishop tried to forbid the people who rallied round him from forming a local *Zoi* affiliated group. The bishop failed. It is natural that some bishops should be suspicious of a large and powerful movement coming to improve the state of religious affairs in their areas of jurisdiction. *A priori* the arrival of a *Zoi* theologian is a suggestion of the diocese's inadequacy.

The unfavourable reaction of the bishops to *Zoi* takes two forms. There is first of all a tiny minority who do all in their power actively to thwart the work of the movement. They usually turn out to be the bishops who have most to fear on account of their own pastoral inadequacies. For example Philip, the former bishop of Drama, in Northern Greece, did all he could to make life difficult for the *Zoi* theologian brother sent to work in his diocese, including forbidding him to preach in any church under his jurisdiction. In 1964 the bishop was found guilty of giving scandal and was dethroned by the Holy Synod. (He had married off a girl, who had lived for some time in the episcopal palace under suspicious circumstances, to a young man, whom he then ordained a priest. The bishop, however, went on seeing the girl, in spite of her marriage.) The dethronement was largely the result of the popular hue and cry raised against the bishop of Drama in which members of the local *Zoi* group took a leading part. Clearly other bishops with skeletons in their cupboards have an interest in keeping their dioceses clear of "*Zoi* busybodies".

The second form of unfavourable episcopal reaction to *Zoi* is to be found among bishops who feel with some justification that the movement cuts diagonally across the traditional vertical system of authority in the diocese. They feel that in effect the local brother takes his orders from the *Zoi* ruling council in Athens and not from the local bishop; through him large numbers of the local middle-class intelligentsia are also controlled by the brotherhood in Athens. These bishops feel that *Zoi* is in some ways forming a Church within the Church, its lay supporters feeling themselves to be first *Zoi* and secondly members of their diocese. Though there is a measure of truth in these criticisms they will only begin to hold water at such time as there is no longer need for outside evangelizing work in the Greek provinces, which as yet is far from being the case. This second group of bishops do not hinder *Zoi's* work in their areas; they merely maintain cool relations with those involved in the work. The more energetic of them try to make *Zoi's* presence unnecessary by themselves organizing catechism classes, sermons, lectures, adult instruction groups and hostels for children from distant villages attending secondary school in the town. As soon as episcopal suspicion of the movement takes this positive turn *Zoi* can feel it has chalked up another success.

There is also a sizeable group of bishops who favour *Zoi's* work and welcome the arrival of a *Zoi* brother in their area. An excellent example of co-operation between a brother and the local bishop is in the see of Didimoticho on the Turkish border. In this case it was the bishop who asked the *Zoi* council to send him a brother to take over the duties of official diocesan preacher priest. There is no apparent friction in this co-operation because the bishop is fully aware that his diocese needs all the help it can get.

It should not be assumed that all middle-class people in Greece are interested in or sympathize with the work of the Brotherhood. Many of them detest its championing of strict moral values and its attacks on their own irreligious way of living—they regard those associated with the movement as bigoted and falsely pietistic. However, as already suggested, *Zoi* has mobilized a fair slice of the bourgeoisie. This is an increasingly important section of the population as prosperity increases and more and more children receive secondary and university education. It is also the section of the population that sets fashions and to which most peasant and working-class parents would like to see their children graduate.

In theory the *Zoi* movement also caters for the peasant farmers and the city workers, but in practice its impact on these two vast sections of the population is very slight. Contact with the villages is restricted to circulation of the *Zoi* magazine, and an annual visit by a *Zoi* brother to some of the larger villages where there are a lot of subscribers to the magazine. The only other way in which the movement has contact with the villages is through the 800 or so primary-school teachers who work in the villages and belong to the Teachers' Association. They take catechism classes, distribute food and parcels of clothes, etc. The time of *Zoi* brothers stationed in the provinces is for the most part taken up with organizing groups in the towns of their area; they do not have time to do anything systematic in the villages.

Though it would be unfair to suggest that *Zoi* has not tried to extend its home mission to the working classes, attempts to date have not met with much success. For example, the magazine put out by the Association of Working Youth has a circulation of only 3,500, one of the lowest of all the *Zoi* affiliated magazines. The Brotherhood's one real success in this sphere is the technical night school in Piraeus attended by 800 boys who want to become skilled workers but do not have the money to pay for a normal night-school course. The boys come to learn a trade, but even the most

thick-skinned can hardly leave at the end of the course without
having been religiously influenced. The reason given by the
brothers themselves for the relative failure to penetrate the
working-class milieu is that opposition and above all apathy to the
faith are stronger there than in any other section of society. A
further reason, however, is the intensely middle-class ethos of the
movement which cannot help but put off the young worker. A
glance at one or two of the dozens of practical little books that
pour off the *Zoi* presses each year makes this quite clear. For
example, the book *Marriage: Harbour or Shipwreck?* deals with
the problems of living together purely in terms of a middle-class
environment. At one point the writer quotes a woman lamenting
how her marriage nearly went to pieces: "When we got married
it never occurred to us that we should tell ourselves: 'Now is the
time to go home.' Instead we carried on as we had lived before
our marriage: going out every evening, worldly company, card-
playing, eating in restaurants, night clubs, dancing, excursions
into the country. Our whole life was spent with other people, never
alone together as husband and wife, as a newly formed family."
The whole of the book is couched in these middle-class terms and
though there are thoughts in it valid for all married couples they
are dressed up in such a way that no working man could possibly
think them relevant to his own situation. The writer has drawn
on his experience as a confessor to middle-class people and his
book is a result of meditation on their particular marriage problems—he has simply not been in contact with the working classes.
This failure of the *Zoi* movement to penetrate the working classes
is largely due to lack of contact and unawareness of their specific
problems.

In the late 'fifties a cleavage occurred inside the *Zoi* Brotherhood between the younger members with progressive ideas and the
older members, including at least one of the 1907 founder members, who were determined that the future policy of the Brother-

hood must follow a strictly traditional line. The immediate cause of the open split between progressives and conservatives that finally occurred in 1960 was over the question of whether the new superior should be elected by democratic vote or appointed by the wish expressed in the will of the previous superior. However, the disagreement went deeper and was really about the *aggiornamento* of the Brotherhood. In June 1960 the fifty conservatives walked out of the *Zoi* house in Athens and set up a new Brotherhood called *Sotir* (Saviour). The lay associations then voted on whether they wanted to stay under *Zoi* or go over to the new *Sotir*. All but one voted in favour of *Zoi*, that is, in favour of the progressives. The single exception was the Parents' Association, made up mainly of older people. At first their defection was a great blow to *Zoi* because most of its real estate all over Greece was in the name of the Parents' Association. It meant that *Zoi* lost its houses, hostels and bookshops in most of the country's provincial towns. In retrospect this has turned out to have been a blessing for it forced the Brotherhood to build smart modern buildings all over Greece in place of the old properties now belonging to *Sotir*, which date back to the 1920s and '30s.

Today *Sotir* has seventy brothers and an identical network of lay associations to that of *Zoi* (built up since 1960, with the exception of the Parents' Association). The magazine *Sotir* sells 70,000 copies, rather more than half of the circulation of the *Zoi* magazine, which gives some idea of its relative influence in the country. The puritanical streak already mentioned as existing in *Zoi* has run riot in the *Sotir* movement. Members of the lay associations may never go to see any film, on the grounds that even if one goes to see the rare good film the atmosphere in cinemas is ungodly and, anyway, one is almost bound to see a scandalizing trailer. The theatre is also regarded with deep suspicion though not condemned as outrightly as the cinema. *Sotir* has taken the idea of repentance and living a clean life to an extreme that reminds one of the excesses of Roundhead England. There is definitely a strong element of latent puritanism in the Greek character and the dour *Sotir* movement reflects it.

Though the break-up of the original *Zoi* community into two different brotherhoods was a painful process and shook the confidence of the lay people connected with the movement it has in the long run been a good thing for the progressives since their hands are no longer tied by internal forces of extreme conservatism. For instance, if *Zoi* still harboured the conservatives who left to form *Sotir*, the brother in Agrinion would never have been given permission to broadcast sermons and book reviews from the local radio station. The conservatives would have argued that it is impious for a religious broadcast to be inserted between two programmes of popular songs.

The indirect influence of *Zoi's* fifty-year-old home mission is to be seen in every corner of Greek ecclesiastical life. Fr John of St Stilianos (mentioned in Chapter 2) was spiritually formed by the movement. The preacher priest in Thebes, Fr Sakelaropoulos, has copied the Brotherhood's system of mobilizing the middle classes by starting lay associations. The three graduate monks who left the Meteora monastery of Barlaam (see Chapter 3) have set themselves up in a house in Athens and are engaged in *Zoi*-type catechizing and preaching. All over the Athens–Piraeus area lay groups have been started on *Zoi* movement lines with the aim of making people live their faith more intelligently and more practically.

In 1947 the success of the Brotherhood's home mission finally brought the hierarchy to set up a home mission of its own, the Apostolic Organization (*Apostoliki Diakonía*). The three main aims of this organization are : (i) to organize sermons all over Greece and to study the techniques of preaching; (ii) to provide training for confessors, and (iii) to organize and supervise a network of catechism classes all over the country. The Apostolic Organization's preaching section is the one that has shown least progress—its main activities are the preparation of a small printed sermon for distribution in all Greek parish churches each Sunday (350,000 printed weekly), and the organization of religious broadcasts for the two national networks. After nearly twenty years it has still not proved possible to publish reference books for preachers; plans to start a preachers' magazine and a preachers' training course have also fallen through. The confessors' section has been more successful and is responsible for the excellent two-month course for country priests held in the Pendeli monastery (see Chapter 1). The area in which the Apostolic Organization has the most positive results to show is in its catechetical work. It runs a six-month course (two hours' instruction a week) for university and training-college students who wish to become catechism teachers—in 1965 there were 170 young people attending this course. To further help catechists in their work it has published twelve large text-books which cover the whole of the nine-year catechism course intended for ten- to eighteen-year-olds.

Though the Apostolic Organization was started by the official Church almost in a spirit of rivalry it now co-operates with both the brotherhoods, *Zoi* and *Sotir*.[2] However its influence on Greek lay people is by no means comparable to theirs. Its well-produced illustrated monthly magazine sells only 15,000 copies in contrast with *Zoi's* 120,000 and *Sotir's* 70,000. This is partly because it was late in the field and there is not an unlimited public wishing to buy religious magazines. The overall impression one gets from sitting in the Organization's offices is that its work is much less carefully and systematically organized than that of the brotherhoods. This is not so much the fault of the priests who work there; it is mainly due to under-staffing and lack of initiative at the top administrative level. Following long and ineffectual squabbling

[2] All *Zoi* and *Sotir* Sunday schools officially come under the Apostolic Organization's wing. Members of both brotherhoods have contributed to the Organization's catechetical books.

in the Holy Synod the organization has been left without a director for the past two and a half years.

The great difference between the movements started by the brotherhoods and the other religious movements in Greece is that while the brotherhoods work as united monastic communities the other movements for the most part depend on the inspiration of one individual. An example of the latter is Fr Kandiotis's movement. He has organized fifteen theologians to live a *Zoi*-style monastic life with preaching, publications and charitable foundations as their main work. In several towns of Northern Greece he has organized hostels for village children attending secondary school and in need of board and lodging. He has set up student hostels in Salonica and Athens. He publishes two magazines. Everything that happens in the movement is done by him or in his name. The movement is generally known as "Fr Kandiotis's Movement". He himself writes every syllable in the 5,000 word monthly magazine *Spitha* (Spark) which is entirely devoted to attacking faults in the Church and in society generally. Fr Kandiotis regards himself as a "protestant" in the Orthodox Church, attacking its present abuses; in his own words, a kind of Savonarola. One month he will attack certain practices of the bishops; another, the plan to found a casino for Swedish tourists on the island of Rhodes; and another, there will be a personal diatribe against a high civil servant in the Ministry of Education and Religion for being an "atheist". He attacks bishops and ministers with comparative impunity but always in a high-pitched, fanatical tone that reduces the credibility of his sometimes justified complaints.

Another example of a one-man movement is that of Fr Nisiotis. Much more level-headed and reasonable than the hot-headed Fr Kandiotis, he has created an organization mainly of lay women and girls who run 300 catechism classes in the Athens area and produce a magazine, *Kainí Ktísis* (New Construction), with a circulation of 3,000. The title of the magazine is significant. Its aim is positive spiritual guidance rather than attack (like *Spitha*). The Nisiotis movement is free of the puritanical streak that is to be found in *Zoi* and even more so in *Sotir*. Fr Nisiotis has not let his movement spread outside the archdiocese of Athens so as not to be open to the charge of meddling in the affairs of other sees. The reasonable and constructive work done by the members of the movement is under the direct inspiration of Fr Nisiotis, and their sensible tone is as much a result of his sympathetic personality as the hectoring tone of the Kandiotis movement is a result of the latter's more bellicose temper. Both movements are the creations of an individual and have as yet failed to develop into community enterprises.

ECUMENISM IN THE BROTHERHOODS AND RELIGIOUS MOVEMENTS

The *Zoi* brothers are nearly all university graduates and some of them are well read in Western spiritual works. A few have had the opportunity to travel abroad and half a dozen or so have studied or are studying in foreign Protestant or Catholic universities. The books published by *Zoi* on the Catholic and Protestant Churches appeared in the late 'fifties and so it is rather unfair to judge the present-day feelings of the brothers towards ecumenism by these two texts since much has happened, ecumenically speaking, in the West since then. On the other hand these books are still prominently displayed in the Brotherhood's bookshops and so read by thousands of ordinary Greek lay people.

The one on Catholicism, entitled *The Western Church*, is largely a re-hash of material from Greek sources—the writer has little direct knowledge of the Catholic Church as it is in fact today. The tone of the book is negative and defensive. For instance, the section describing the differences between the two Churches is headed: "Her errors" (the Catholic Church's), and opens like this: "From the period when the Western Church cut herself off from the One, Holy, Catholic and Apostolic Church, that is to say the Orthodox Church, her errors have multiplied and hardened into permanence. . . ." The choice of example in the book is loaded and misleading. For example, to illustrate the pride of the Papal institution the author quotes titles like "*dominus dominorum*" *and* "*ordinarius singulorum*" but makes no mention of the Pope's perhaps most common title "*servus servorum Dei*". He frequently describes situations which were current and abominable in Catholicism four centuries ago but which no longer exist today. He gives a picture of papal indulgences being bought by wealthy Catholics which would do justice to the pen of a sixteenth-century reformer. The writer's conclusion in 1959 about hopes of *rapprochement* between Rome and the Orthodox was: "It does not seem that the hour has yet struck for the Western Church to approach the question of reunion in a spirit of humility and sincerity and with a truly holy disposition. . . ."

The *Zoi* book on the Protestants, by the author of *The Western Church*, is conceived in a substantially different spirit. Though the "errors" of the Protestant Churches are condemned as, and even more roundly than, those of Rome, the author sees concrete proof of *rapprochement* between them and Orthodoxy. He writes: "It is both pleasing and encouraging that a movement should have started in Europe among the Protestants for a return to the ancient sources of the faith and for a *rapprochement* with Orthodoxy . . . many Protestants feel nostalgia for a conscious sacramental life as taught by our Orthodox Church. Driven by this deep desire they are trying to lay better dogmatic foundations and to start a liturgical and monastic movement. . . ."

Although the dogmatic and doctrinal differences between the Orthodox and the Protestants are much greater than those between the Orthodox and the Catholics, the author feels that the disposition of the Protestants is better than that of the Catholics. The former almost show signs of wishing to return to the Orthodox fold, at any rate as seen from Greece, while the latter have the impertinence to invite the Orthodox to return to their fold. The Protestants do not seem proud, to the Orthodox, in the way the Catholics do.

The influence of the *Zoi* books on Catholicism and Protestantism is not confined to those who read them directly. Both books have been used as main source works for the chapters on non-Orthodox Christian Churches in the catechism text-books of the Apostolic Organization. These text-books are used by catechists all over Greece in preparing their lessons and it is particularly unfortunate that the country's late-teenagers should be taught from texts as unecumenical as this one (an extract from the chapter: "The Superiority of Orthodoxy over Catholicism"): ". . . We must not cease praying for the union of all the Churches, that is to say the return of the Western Church to the Orthodox East. . . . The Roman Catholic Church must become deeply conscious of her guilt and must sincerely repent for all the suffering she has caused the Orthodox Church in the past. She must collaborate wisely and humbly so as to produce an atmosphere of mutual respect. When this happens we must forgive those who did us wrong. We must be drawn to the reunion of the Churches by the understanding and union of our souls." The visual aids for this lesson suggested at the end of the chapter are "films and slides which show the dark as well as the good side of the Roman Catholic Church".

By 1965 the attitude of the *Zoi* Brotherhood to the Catholic Church had definitely progressed from the negative stand taken by the author of the 1959 book on *The Western Church*. The editorial reaction of the magazine *Zoi* to the January 1964 Pope–Patriarch meeting was as follows: "The duty imposed on the Orthodox man in the street by this meeting is to pray for the dialogue that has been begun. It is the duty of the theologians to embark on a

D

systematic study of the questions at stake and to ensure that close co-operation is achieved not only between the theological faculties of Athens, Salonica, Halki, and Boston [Greek ones] but also with the Russian Institutes of New York and Paris and the Balkan theological schools. . . . We cannot allow ourselves to be left behind at a time when the Roman Church is taking considerable steps towards self-renewal by means of study and councils. Orthodoxy should be Christ's servant and the light of Christ in the ecumenical dialogue. . . ." The burden of this editorial is echoed in conversation with individual *Zoi* brothers. Their preoccupation is that, in view of the new hand of friendship that Rome has extended, the Orthodox Church as a whole, both Greek and Slav cycles, should put their houses in order and be ready to face theological dialogue with Rome. Most of them, however, feel that the internal spring-cleaning of Orthodox theology must be the work of the university faculties—their work is the home mission and they cannot take on anything else. This new attitude in the *Zoi* Brotherhood is most promising ecumenically speaking since, as already pointed out, they wield considerable influence in the country's leading class, the bourgeoisie.

The *Sotir* Brotherhood has taken up a much more conservative and unecumenical stand than *Zoi's*. A book published by *Sotir* in 1964 shows the difference of attitude even in its title, *The Misbeliefs of Papism*. The author feels that the first two sessions of Vatican II showed there has been little progress in Catholic ecumenical thinking, since the primacy and infallibility of the Pope have been reaffirmed. The style of the book is polemic, as this extract shows: "In a speech he made at the opening of the third session of the Vatican Council Pope Paul VI reasserted the inadmissible conceptions held by the Roman Catholic Church of the primacy and infallibility of the Pope, conceptions which are contrary to tradition. He did not hesitate to re-state his 'absolute primacy' and to speak of himself as 'the latest successor of the

Apostle Peter, invested with the same authority and bearing the same responsibility as Peter'." The author's conclusion is that it was egoism that produced the schism, which could easily have been bridged in the past had the popes not dreamt of becoming monarchs with the whole world bowing before them. "Once egoism has been laid aside then there will be very little difficulty in effecting reunion. This can only come about when those who have put a distance between themselves and the truth return to the truth and when those who have strayed from the traditions of the Apostles and Fathers recognize their mistake." The writer goes on to qualify the "errors" of Rome as not just schismatic but heretical. Though *Sotir* has considerable influence among older people, especially in the middle classes, a book like *The Misbeliefs of Papism* often preaches to the converted. It may strengthen a view of Rome already held but is unlikely to make an ecumenically progressive person renounce his views and become a conservative.

The most ecumenically minded religious movement in Greece is probably that of Fr Nisiotis. His magazine *Kainí Ktísis* regularly carries an article on what is going on in the West and its comments on the work of the Vatican Council always showed comprehension of what was happening there. Even if, from an Orthodox angle, something said or done in the Council was unpalatable, *Kainí Ktísis* tried to put the matter in its real perspective. This is how the magazine commented on Pope Paul's speech at the opening of the third session : "It is clear that in many of the points made in his speech the Pontiff was this time much more Roman than on previous occasions. The two unshakeable premises on which his whole discourse was based were papal primacy and the concept that full truth is only to be found in the Roman Catholic Church. Many Catholic theologians felt bitter about this. Some suggested that Paul VI was not, in all the points he made, expressing his own opinion but that he was in a difficult position owing to strong internal opposition from the Vatican. He himself would have preferred to avoid so Roman a stand, but it was clearly not yet time to take more steps forward, as he himself would like."

In its comprehension of the difficulties attending Catholicism's *aggiornamento*, Fr Nisiotis's magazine is pretty well unique among Greek Orthodox publications. One of the reasons for Fr Nisiotis's strongly ecumenical attitude is that he is kept fully informed as to what goes on abroad by his theologian son, Nikos Nisiotis, who was a World Council of Churches' observer at the third session of the Vatican Council. The magazine has only a small circulation (3,000), but Fr Nisiotis's influence goes well beyond this narrow radius. Nine of today's fifty-five or so bishops passed through his hands when they were young either as confessees or as members of the movement. This does not mean that they are all ecumenically minded men today but at any rate they will have been given an idea of what ecumenism is. One of them, Mgr Damaskinos of Volos (Dimitriados), is perhaps the most ecumenically minded bishop in Greece.

In ecumenical matters the influence of Fr Kandiotis and his movement is just the opposite to that of Fr Nisiotis. In the January 1964 number of *Spitha* Fr Kandiotis attacked the Patriarch fiercely and insultingly for his meeting with the Pope. He described ecumenism as a sweet sounding word, "but under cover of this word lies hidden the most dreadful danger to Orthodoxy." He compared Orthodoxy to an actress seen by thousands of eyes but ever faithful to her husband (Christ). Many men desire her and approach her, but because she is honourable and faithful she rebuffs them all. But then some of them try a new method : they talk to her about things she likes, such as poetry, the theatre, music, and she is drawn into conversation forgetting that what they are really after is her virtue, ". . . and then when the conversation has produced a climate of intimacy and mutual understanding, then follows the fatal, dishonourable act, the disgusting union which started as an innocent dialogue." He goes on to describe Rome as the enemy of Orthodoxy, reunion as "spiritual adultery" and such Orthodox as work towards reunion as "pimps". In interviewing Fr Kandiotis I asked him why he could not set out his views on the dangers of *rapprochement* with Rome in civil language. He replied : "No, it is not possible to write courteously. There is need for bitterness to arouse the people to the danger. As yet we have no real proof of a change of heart on the part of Rome and into the bargain we are quite unprepared for a dialogue, morally, intellec-ectually and organizationally. . . . As a whole Orthodoxy is in no state to meet the well-trained and well-organized theologians of the West." I suggested that there was no need to be rude to Rome on account of Orthodoxy's own internal weaknesses. He disagreed. He said *Spitha* must be extreme in its expression because there is a great weight of opinion in Greece today in favour of reunion. Workers who go abroad to Germany, for instance, see good Catholic priests and compare them with the bad ones at home in Greece; they come to feel that if the Pope is their leader he cannot be such a bad man after all. Fr Kandiotis told me that the Greeks are losing their traditional fear of Catholicism and that this is dangerous for Orthodoxy at the present time.

Though *Spitha* prints 30,000 copies a month its true subscriber circulation is less, since a large number of copies are given away at Fr Kandiotis's frequent public protest meetings. It has a certain following owing to the latent fanaticism of the Greeks and because Fr Kandiotis, for all his extremism, has the reputation of being a holy and courageous man. His chief significance in the ecumenical sphere is that he has the ear of Archbishop Chrysostomos of Athens and the hard kernel of anti-ecumenical bishops who are the Arch-bishop's chief supporters in the Greek hierarchy. His influence and that of other pressure groups on the ageing Archbishop will be examined in the next chapter.

5
the bishops

THE BISHOPS of the Orthodox Church of Greece are men invested with great power and consequently they carry great responsibilities. As a body, in the assembly of the full hierarchy, they constitute the final authority in the autocephalous Church of Greece. The authority of the Ecumenical Patriarch of Constantinople in Orthodoxy can in no way be compared to the Pope's authority in Catholicism—the Patriarch has no say whatsoever in the decisions taken by the hierarchy of an autocephalous Church, while, on the other hand, when *he* acts in the name of world Orthodoxy his actions must be approved by the separate hierarchies of all the autocephalous Orthodox Churches. In other words, the episcopal assemblies of the autocephalous Churches are the final arbiters of what world Orthodoxy will or will not do.

As all the day-to-day questions that come up cannot and need not be discussed by the full hierarchy, these are dealt with by the Holy Synod, a body made up of the Archbishop of Athens and twelve other bishops. The twelve bishops serve for a year and then are replaced by another twelve, the only permanent member of the Synod being the Archbishop of Athens. As a result of this system each Greek bishop spends one year in five away from his diocese, sitting as a member of the Synod in Athens.

It must regretfully be said that at the present time the Synod is a remarkably inefficient instrument of Church government. An instance of its inefficiency is the way it has left the Apostolic Organization (see Chapter 4) without a director for more than two years, although the matter is periodically brought up and argued about.

The Synod's inefficiency is not entirely its own fault, since it works within the framework of an uneasy *modus vivendi* between the Church and the State. Orthodoxy is the country's official religion, but the price the Church pays for this official status is its independence. The constitutional charter of the Church, which is periodically altered and brought up to date, has to be amended by committees of bishops, lay theologians, and civil servants from the Ministry of Education and Religion. The amendments are then passed as a bill through the national parliament. Financially the Church is in no position to claim her independence, since the State pays the salaries of the parish clergy and into the bargain heavily subsidizes the Church's own budget.

The dependence of Church on State makes for friction at all levels. Friction at grass-roots level occurs, for instance, when the employees of the State Archaeological Service clean the frescoes in a historic monastery church and then forbid the monks to sing divine office there on the ground that smoke from their candles would make the frescoes dirty again (Osios Loukas). Most of the frictions between Church and State come to a head in the relations between the Holy Synod, or the assembled hierarchy, and the Ministry of Education and Religion or Parliament. In 1963 Parliament passed a law on the compilation of the list of episcopal candidates and the transfer of bishops from see to see. (There were at that time ten sees vacant.) The law forbade the filling of a large, rich see by transfer of a bishop from another, smaller see, except in the case of the archbishopric of Athens. The Synod decided to pass the matter over to the assembly of the hierarchy, which immediately denounced the law as anti-canonical and anti-constitutional and declared that this was yet another instance of State interference in Church affairs. On 7 October 1963, the hierarchy decided by thirty-eight votes to six to postpone the filling of the ten vacant sees until after Parliament had voted on the amendments to the Church's constitutional charter, then in preparation. Two years later Church and State had still not agreed on the question of transferring bishops from see to see. By November 1965 fifteen sees were vacant and a majority of the hierarchy (thirty-six bishops against fifteen) decided on drastic action : they defied an injunction by the Supreme Council of State[1] and proceeded to fill the fifteen sees, two of them by episcopal transfer. The minority of fifteen bishops did not take part in the elections and declared them illegal and uncanonical. The Government took the same view and refused the royal decree on which the appointment of the new bishops depends. At the time of writing (December 1965) the crisis remains unresolved with the Government adamantly refusing to appoint the fifteen new bishops, who had, however, been duly consecrated. The crisis came to a head largely because of the bishops' understandable anger at the Government's dilatory interference in Church affairs. A graphic expression of this anger came in an exchange between Mgr Chrysostomos of Argolis and Prime Minister Stephanopoulos on 16 November 1965. The Prime Minister warned Mgr Chrysostomos that the election of new bishops in defiance of the Supreme Council of State would be null and void, to which the bishop replied : "Don't you shake your finger at me. We are the representatives of the hierarchy, you are one of the flock—you are nothing!"

Besides taking part in the administration of the Church on a national scale each bishop is the *despótis* in his own diocese. *Despótis* (despot), which is the normal word local people use in

[1] The Papandreou Government agreed that the seven largest sees in Greece should be filled by transfer. In autumn 1965 the Stephanopoulos Cabinet decided that two sees plus the archbishopric of Athens should be filled by transfer. In October Bishop Ambrosios of Eleutheroupolis appealed against this Cabinet decision to the Supreme Council of State (*Simvoulion tis Epikrateias*). The Council issued an injunction suspending the Cabinet decision and postponing the episcopal elections until it had judged Mgr Ambrosios's appeal. This was the injunction which the thirty-six bishops defied and which the fifteen, led by Mgr Ambrosios, upheld by not attending the election.

referring to the bishop, is a title which in Byzantine times was given only to a temporal ruler but which during the Turkish occupation was applied to the bishops, since the Ottomans held them responsible for the civil administration of the local Christians. Though in theory the bishop is answerable for what he does to the Holy Synod and in the final resort to an ecclesiastical court (made up of his peers), unless he gives considerable scandal (as was the case with the Bishop of Drama, see Chapter 4) he is fully master in his own diocese. The predecessor to the present bishop of Eleutheroupolis, Mgr Sempronios, demanded impossibly high standards of spirituality from men wishing to become parish priests. If they did not satisfy these standards he refused to ordain them and as a result half the villages in his diocese had no priests. Such was his policy; he was the *despótis* and that was that.

With the exception of the three large sees of Athens (nearly one and a half million), Piraeus (half a million) and Salonica (400,000), the average Greek diocese counts only 86,000 souls. This average is deceptive since there are quite a number of dioceses with only 50,000 or so people in them and one even comes across a few bishops in the islands and remote upland areas with flocks of 30,000 and less. The smallest see in Greece is Kythira with 5,500 souls. As people migrate to the towns and abroad the smaller, less prosperous diocese tends to shrink still further. A principal result of the smallness of the diocese is that the bishop is able to rule his particular area down to the very last detail. He is not a distant ethereal figure protected by phalanxes of vicars-general and secretaries—if he does his job properly he is in a very direct sense the pastor of the people and the arbiter of the lives of the clergy. The aura of power round the bishop is enhanced by the mingled fear and respect which the uneducated or at the most half-educated clergy feel for him. They come to the bishop to ask permission to do things more educated men would do off their own bat. Into the bargain the parish clergy regard him as the guarantor of their livings—it was the bishop who promised them a parish before they went to the seminary and it is he who will dismiss them if he is not satisfied with them. In seven of the twenty Greek dioceses I have visited, apart from the vicar-general and the preacher priest, the bishop was the only graduate theologian in the diocese. It is frequently asserted, in non-episcopal ecclesiastical circles, that certain bishops prefer their parish clergy to be uneducated as it is easier to rule today's uneducated priests autocratically than it would be were they theologians. This much can be said : a local priest of little education is less likely to criticize his bishop effectively than a theology graduate who during his four-year university course in Salonica or Athens will have made a number of influential contacts. It is also said that bishops often refuse to ordain educated men whom they think might criticize them in the future. I have not been able to unearth any concrete, authenticated case of this happening, but given the general state of the Greek episcopate today it would not be surprising if there were some truth in the charge.

A further factor that tends to concentrate all local administrative power in the hands of the bishop is the generalized Greek habit of shuffling decision making on to the shoulders of one's immediate superior. This phenomenon is observable in all Government services and goes a long way towards explaining the self-strangulation of the Greek bureaucracy. It happens in diocesan administration too —the vicar-general avoids taking all but the most minor decisions and in effect his role is often that of a superior sort of secretary. The exception to this is in cases where the bishop is very old and decrepit.

A good example of an effective Greek *despótis* is Mgr Barnabas[2]

[2] The general Greek word for bishop is *"epískopos"*, but a bishop with a diocese (as opposed to an auxiliary bishop) has the title *"Mitropolítis"*. Since this title has no Western equivalent I refer to bishops as "Mgr X" or as "Mgr X of Y", or "Bishop X of Y".

of Ekaterini (Kitrous). He is a better educated man than most of his peers, holding degrees in both law and theology and having done post-graduate theological studies in Boston. (All Greek bishops have to be theology graduates but few of them have done post-graduate studies.) Mgr Barnabas takes his supervisory duties very seriously and makes full use of his car and chauffeur to get round his sixty or so villages as frequently as possible. He is not satisfied with being surrounded by uneducated clergy, and when he arrived in 1954 he started a seminary for turning out third-class priests which has since come up in the world and turns out second-class ones. As a result there are now almost no empty parishes in his diocese. He has three preachers instead of the normal one, two of them priests and one a layman. He has sent one of them for post-graduate studies to England. When I visited him he had no vicar-general. The second-class priest who normally carried out these duties had been sent to Salonica University to acquire a theology degree.

Mgr Barnabas feels that a bishop should not be just an administrator and a supervisor of the clergy, he should also take his duties as a priest seriously. To this end he has revived episcopal vespers in the local cathedral and every Saturday night the people gather for vespers and to hear the bishop preach. The Saturday I went, though it was pouring with rain, about 700 dripping people came to listen to a sermon on the need for frequent communion. The sermon had obviously been carefully thought out—the bishop told me afterwards that he was very much preoccupied with the difficulties of holding an audience so mixed as to include primary-school children and members of the town's intelligentsia. He has paid great attention to organizing catechism classes in the diocese. There are at the moment one hundred of them with 5,000 pupils (the population of the diocese is 100,000). He also runs a diocesan magazine to counter the influence of the local paper run by the town's Evangelical minority. Since he became bishop in 1954 he has built a new bishop's house, the seminary, two youth centres, one for boys and one for girls, a spiritual centre for adults which includes a lecture hall, cinema and library, a kindergarten for children with mothers who work, and a housewifery school in one of the villages of the diocese.

Though there is no doubt that Bishop Barnabas (in his fifties) is aware of the spiritual needs of the area and does not spare himself in satisfying them, he is also very definitely a *despótis* and does not easily brook opposition to his authority. The Town Council of Ekaterini, for example, wanted to make a public square out of a plot of land on which the bishop had decided to build his spiritual centre for adults. Quite illegally Mgr Barnabas walked into a meeting of the Town Council and warned them to take their hands off God's land. As a result of his unconstitutional intervention the bishop carried the day and the Council decided by a few votes to leave the plot to the Church. Bishop Barnabas is also at pains that the rest of Greece should not be ignorant of the good work that is going on in the diocese of Ekaterini—to enlighten opinion in the country he has produced an expensive brochure with photographs of the new diocesan buildings. Better use could perhaps have been found for this money. However, given the really good work he is doing, it would be petty to cavil too much over the streaks of ambition and autocracy apparent in Mgr Barnabas's character. As a bishop in the provincial Greek situation he is up to a point expected to behave as a "despot".

Mgr Barnabas is typical of a number of bishops elected in the fifties who share two essential common denominators: comparative youthfulness and energy. The latter is absolutely necessary to the running of the average Greek diocese made up of tiny villages, each one up a different cul-de-sac in the mountains. The diocese of Naupaktos illustrates the need for episcopal stamina. The bishop, Mgr Damaskinos, has in his care 50,000 people living in 180 villages, of which only seven can be easily reached from the diocesan town. To get to the other 173, which lie to the north of a chain of high mountains, the bishop has to go on a circumventing road journey of five hours before he even reaches a centre from which he can start visiting. This particular bishop is young and enthusiastic and though he does not have a car he manages to get around to even the remotest villages.

The episcopate falls into disrepute when bishops who are too old or too ill to carry out their duties insist on staying on instead of allowing themselves to be pensioned off. A case in point is Mgr Dorotheos of Thebes and Levadeia. The townspeople of Levadeia late in 1964 signed a petition asking him to resign, but he refused to. The Synod even tried to coax him into resigning by offering him a pension equal to his present salary and half again if he would resign willingly instead of having to be removed on grounds of ill-health. He still refused and at the time of writing the matter is still pending. The only village parishes which the aged bishop visits regularly are those to which he has sent new young priests, as he evidently thinks that supervision is most needful when a young priest has just taken on a parish. There are some villages in the diocese that he has not got round to visiting more than once in his six-year reign. This kind of neglect, be its cause physical incapacity on the part of the bishop, or indifference, breeds indiscipline among the clergy and religious apathy among the villagers : "if the *despótis* can't even come to see us every two or three years . . .".

Another case of a bishop really no longer capable of carrying his responsibilities was the nonagenarian Bishop of Hydra, Mgr Prokopios, who apart from looking after his own sparsely populated group of islands, was in charge, from 1962 till 1965, of the vacant see of Piraeus, with its half a million population. In Chapter 2 we looked into some of the problems that confront the Church in the vast sprawl of the Athens–Piraeus area and it is no depreciation of Mgr Prokopios, who served the Church faithfully as a bishop from 1912, to suggest that at the age of ninety-five he was not the right man to be bishop of Piraeus.[3]

Though Western style anti-clericalism does not exist in Greece (i.e., the feeling against the cassock as such), there is a rising wave of dissatisfaction with the bishops, both among people indifferent to the Church and among practising Orthodox. This dissatisfaction is with the personal standards of the bishops and their ineffectual performance in the Holy Synod. When one talks to preacher priests in the provinces they often let on in a more or less round-about way that their local bishop leaves much to be desired. In conversation with people affiliated to the various religious movements (*Zoi*, *Sotir*, *Kandiotis*, etc.) one is often told of the lack of spirituality among the bishops. There is a widespread popular feeling that the bishops are in it mainly for the money. Many people feel that this is why the Synod is so anxious that large vacant sees like Piraeus should be filled by transfer of another bishop from a smaller diocese. In this way, the popular explanation runs, the men who are already bishops in poor areas will take over sees with vast incomes and be able to live in the lap of luxury. There may be some truth in this explanation, but the Synod and the hierarchy's determination to maintain the right to transfer bishops from see to see must also be seen as a stand taken against high-handed State legislation forbidding such transfers and in the light of the Synod's own explanation of its stand, namely that the administration of a big see like Piraeus requires experience that only a man who has already been a bishop for some years can have.

Where there's smoke there's fire and the popular feeling against the episcopate is based on some of the less than edifying actions of the bishops themselves. Even when a bishop does visit a parish in his diocese it is not always with the aim of supervising the priest and preaching to the people, as it should be. Often he goes at the request of an individual to celebrate a marriage, for which service

[3] Mgr Prokopios died on 3 December 1965.

he is paid, as an ordinary priest would be, but in accordance with his rank—in other words he rakes in a much higher fee. I have even come across the case of a bishop who, when asked to come and consecrate a newly-built village church, demanded that the village should pay him £35 for his trouble. Unlike the parish priests the bishops are not forced into accepting "luck-money" by the inadequacy of their salaries. They are paid the same salary as a High Court judge or an M.P. (about £3,600 per annum; and Greek income tax is much lighter than the English). All their travelling and living expenses are covered from the diocesan budget. The diocese's income comes from a percentage levy on all money raised by the parishes (sales of candles, marriage licences, etc.) and a percentage from the income of the local monasteries and their properties. This latter is sometimes a source of considerable sums.

In the Western Churches the bishops are picked from among the holiest, most learned, most administratively capable or best connected members of the clergy. In the Greek Orthodox Church a normal member of the parish clergy cannot rise to episcopal rank, since the normal Orthodox parish priest is a married man while the bishop has to be celibate. In practice this means that the young man leaving the theological faculty with a priestly vocation must decide whether to marry and become a life-long parish priest or whether to remain celibate and hope for a crozier. If he is a university-trained theologian and does stay celibate he has a good chance of ending up as a bishop. In the meantime he will either get himself a job as a vicar-general, a celibate parish priest in one of the central Athenian churches, or a preacher priest in the provinces. It sometimes happens that a theology graduate waits to be ordained until a friend of his becomes a bishop and can take him on as vicar-general. This sort of ordinand has obviously set his sights fairly and squarely on the acquisition at a later date of a see of his own. The same goes for celibate priests with parishes in central Athens

—they tell one quite openly that they missed a bishopric at the last episcopal elections by, say, three votes but that they should be successful next time. The 140 preacher priests scattered round the Greek provinces have chosen the hardest and holiest way to a bishopric. There are certainly some of them who are not ambitious at all and would be quite content with going on preaching and confessing without acquiring a throne. These 140 men are among the hardest worked and most devoted members of the Greek clergy, facing as they do intellectual exile in small provincial towns, their week taken up with catechism classes and confession, and their week-ends, winter and summer, devoted to going to remote villages which may be four or five hours away by bus and mule. Unlike the bishops, the preacher priests never have cars. The more bishops come from among their ranks and the less from among the vicars-general and central Athenian celibate parish clergy the better it will be for the future of the Greek episcopate.

THE GREEK BISHOPS AND ROME

The views of the Greek bishops on recent developments in Rome must be seen in the light of the inadequate sources of information at their disposal. The coverage the Greek dailies gave the Vatican Council was limited to factual reports often not exceeding a dozen lines of newspaper column print. The only events in the third session to get substantial treatment were the opening ceremonies and the row over the religious liberty draft. The average Greek bishop is psychologically inclined to feel that the most trustworthy sources of information on happenings in Rome are *Ekklisia* (the official journal of the Church of Greece, controlled by the highly anti-ecumenical Archbishop of Athens) and *Anaplasis*. A typical example of the scanty treatment accorded to Catholic affairs in the religious press was the report in *Ekklisia* on 15 December 1964 entitled: "The Conclusion of the Third Session of the Vatican

Synod". The 180-word report contained only one fact: that the Vatican Council had almost unanimously voted in favour of the ecumenical draft "which contains many enlightened points". No hint was given of the content of the ecumenical decree. The rest of the report was comment, most of it unfavourable. *Katholiki*,[4] the weekly newspaper brought out by the Uniats, is the only fully adequate Greek language source of information on Catholic affairs, but feeling against the Uniats runs high and only a number of the more open-minded bishops take their paper. A theologian priest I met in Western Greece does not dare to receive *Katholiki* directly through the post for fear of what people might say. He has it sent

---

[4] *Katholiki* is the organ of the Uniats. There are at the moment about twenty Greek-rite Catholic priests in Greece ministering to about 2,500 faithful in two parishes, one in Athens and one in Northern Greece (the Latin-rite Catholics number about 40,000). Unlike the ancient Uniat Churches of the Near East (the Melkites, etc.) the Uniats of Greece have only been an organized ecclesiastical body for a little over forty years—the Greek-rite Catholics of Constantinople became an organized ecclesiastical body in 1912 with the appointment by the Vatican of a bishop and they transferred to Greece at the time of the Greek exodus from Turkey in 1922–24. In the 1920s and '30s the Greek Uniats were, by their own admission, engaged in active proselytism. Since the war proselytism has in fact stopped, but the Orthodox find this hard to believe especially when they see the Uniats' social work: a modern hospital, an orphanage, student hostels, etc. . . . These foundations of necessity cater mainly for Orthodox people. All the Greek Orthodox bishops whose views I have heard or read and all the university theologians of Greece, with two possible exceptions, condemn the Uniats out of hand and regard them as Catholics dressed up like Orthodox pappádes, luring the Orthodox faithful into services which outwardly exactly resemble Orthodox services but which in fact are not. In 1927 the then Archbishop of Athens, Mgr Chrysostomos, wrote in a letter to the first bishop of the Uniats of Greece: "We feel that the Greek rite of Catholicism, which you represent, is simply a pretext, a fraudulent device for proselytizing simple Orthodox folk. Uniatism and its history bears witness to this, has caused great scandal wherever it has appeared. . . ." These words, written in 1927, are still an accurate representation of the views of the majority of the Orthodox theologians and the totality of the episcopate of Greece in 1965.

by a friend in a disguised wrapper. A handful of bishops who read
languages other than Greek follow developments in Rome directly
through foreign Catholic magazines. Not many Greek bishops are
able to read foreign languages.

Mgr Dorotheos of Thebes and Levadeia is a fair example of the
minority of bishops who are openly hostile towards Rome and find
recent ecumenically directed developments inside Catholicism of
little interest. He told me that "understanding" with Rome could
only mean the "submission" of Orthodoxy. Rome must first of all
show that she has changed her attitude in matters of substance and
not just content herself with gestures like the return of the Apostle
Andrew's head to Patras. If Rome were to renounce her errors
there would not even be need for a dialogue, "but we have learnt
from our history that Rome's friendship is a Trojan Horse. When
I think back to the Crusades . . .".

On the whole those hostile to Rome tend to have some idea of
what is going on there. In contrast to them are the bishops who
are innocent of all knowledge on ecumenical questions, like Mgr
Dorotheos of Leucas. He is seventy-seven and has been looking
after the island of Leucas, which is little more than a very large
rural parish (36,000 souls) since 1940. His eyes are bad and he can
only just read. It was not possible to discuss his reactions to the
decisions of the third session of the Vatican Council because he
simply had not heard about them. In the sleepy island town from
which Mgr Dorotheos administers his diocese this absence of
knowledge did not seem shocking, but one year in every five he
spends in Athens sitting in the twelve-member Synod which
decides questions such as whether or not observers should be sent
to Rome. Seen from this angle, his ignorance is more worrying. It
is not merely the very old who are uninformed: the young and
vigorous Mgr Ignatios of Arta was under the quite mistaken
impression that Greece had sent observers to the third session of
the Vatican Council, and he was a member of the 1964–65 Synod.

I have mentioned the bishops who are openly hostile to ecumenism and those who are unaware of what is going on abroad. A third category comprises those who are well informed but who for all that see little hope of *rapprochement* with Rome. Mgr Barnabas of Ekaterini (Kitrous) follows Anglican events in the *Church Times* and Catholic affairs in *Katholiki* and various French periodicals. Asked for his views on the third session, he said that Pope Paul seems to take two or three little steps forward and then one large one backwards. He quoted *Ecclesiam suam* and other recent affirmations of papal primacy as examples of steps backward. Mgr Barnabas explained that the Pope was obliged to do this by cross-currents inside Catholicism, but that his statements amount to barometer readings of the climate in the Catholic Church as a whole.

Half a dozen of the fifty-five or so Greek bishops can be classed as ecumenically minded. Mgr Damaskinos of Volos (Dimitriados) is one of the most outspoken of their number. He learnt his ecumenism as a p.o.w. in Italy and later in Dachau. He keeps informed of Catholic developments through correspondence with his many Western friends, among whom is Cardinal Bea, and by reading the *Osservatore Romano* and various German and French periodicals. In the summer of 1962, just before the opening of the first session of the Vatican Council, he had a one-and-a-half-hour conversation with Pope John. This caused a considerable wave of hostile reaction among his fellow bishops in Greece. Mgr Damaskinos would very much liked to have been in Rome during the fourth session as a "friend", though his position as a bishop would have made it difficult for him to go as such unofficially. He was wary of commenting on the third session but agreed when I said that some progressive Catholics were disappointed by some of the session's decisions.

The feeling among the ecumenically-minded bishops is that the Greek hierarchy as a whole is not against contact with Rome out of any deep conviction but because they are either unaware of what is going on there or are purposefully misinformed by a vocal minority of hostile bishops led by the Archbishop of Athens who are in their turn strongly influenced by a number of pressure groups, the most important of which are those led by Fr Kandiotis (*Spitha*) and Abbot Vasilopoulos of the Petraki monastery, in central Athens. Abbot Vasilopoulos has considerable influence over the Archbishop. He was late for my interview with him because the Archbishop had held him up, and is even more extremist in his view of the Catholic Church than Fr Kandiotis. The January 1964 issue of his monthly paper *Typos* carried a photo of the Pope and the Patriarch arm in arm during their Jerusalem meeting with this caption underneath : "The Pope holds his prey [the Patriarch] like a hyena, with an expression of savage delight on his face. A feeling of deep guilt is reflected in Athenagoras's embarrassed gaze." Without agreeing with nonsense of this fanatical sort, many monoglot bishops are influenced by the climate of distrust it produces. The most amazing thing is that Archbishop Chrysostomos and a group of four or five other bishops and several abbots from various monasteries in Greece and on Athos go along with Vasilopoulos. On the night before the meeting of the Pope and the Patriarch the Archbishop attended part of an all-night vigil in the Petraki monastery held "against the meeting".

The Archbishop has considerable power as the permanent chairman of a Synod whose members come and go each year. As chairman he can delay the discussion of topics he prefers to avoid and can withhold, at least for a time, information sent to him but intended to be shared with the other members of the Synod. He and his sympathizers have had it largely their own way in the last three or four years and have managed to project an image of the Greek Church abroad which is much more anti-ecumenical than the reality. If the Synod one year happens to be made up of bishops who have little contact with ecumenical problems, most of them adopt the attitude expressed to me by Bishop Iakovos of Larissa, who said he refuses to judge ecumenical events abroad until he has heard the views and comments of his fellow bishops. In a Synod of this sort the bishops are the sheep and the anti-ecumenical Archbishop is the shepherd. When there is a definitely ecumenically-minded bishop in the Synod, as there was in the 1964–65 Synod (Mgr Panteleimon of Salonica), he provides a counterweight to the views of the Archbishop and stands as a leader around whom some of the more open-minded but uninformed bishops can rally.

A clear example of the swing inside the Synod that even one ecumenically-minded bishop can produce was the change in composition of the Greek delegation to the third Pan-Orthodox Conference. In the summer of 1964 the Archbishop had the sort of Synod he wanted—not only were there no particularly ecumenically-minded bishops in it but there was one, Mgr Chrysostomos of Argolis, who was almost as anti-ecumenical as himself. The Synod was duly persuaded to choose a five-man delegation to be sent to the Conference, with Argolis at its head. So far so good—Greece was to be represented by a basically anti-ecumenical delegation at a conference called by the Patriarch of Constantinople to discuss the start of a dialogue with the Catholic Church. But in October 1964, just before the Conference, a new Synod had to be convened and one of its members was Mgr Panteleimon of Salonica. Within two weeks the five-man delegation had been expanded to eight and Salonica had replaced Argolis as its head. The other two new members were both ecumenically disposed men. Argolis was so peeved that he resigned from the delegation.

It would be quite wrong to underestimate the power that the reactionary bishops and pressure groups wield. The Greek hierarchy as a whole is still too ignorant of what goes on abroad to react against the distorted views which the pressure groups are intent on broadcasting of the Catholic Church and of the ecumenically-minded Constantinople hierarchy led by Patriarch Athenagoras. It must, on the other hand, be remembered that the reactionaries for the moment hold a trump card in the person of the ageing Mgr Chrysostomos. The Archbishop personally controls the Church's official journal and can, up to a point, manipulate the Synod, both technically as its chairman and through the prestige of his position. A great deal in the future will depend on whom the successor to the octogenarian Chrysostomos turns out to be; at all events, since Mgr Chrysostomos is Greece's most consistently anti-ecumenical bishop, his successor cannot help but have a somewhat mellower attitude.

[The statistics in this chapter concerning bishops refer to the situation before November 1965 when fifteen new bishops were elected.]

6

intellectuals of orthodoxy:
the lay theologians

A BASIC DIFFERENCE between Orthodoxy and Catholicism is the place given to the *Laós*, the people. Like the Catholics, the Orthodox think of the priest as the shepherd and the people as the flock, but the Orthodox do not push the comparison so hard as to come to regard lay people as sheep under the absolute religious rule of the clergy. The *Laós* is thought of in Orthodoxy as having an active part to play in the Church's life. For instance, the final rightness or wrongness of any doctrinal decision taken by an assembly of bishops is judged by whether in the long run the people accept the decision or not. The Catholic concept that the Church defines and the people in obedience submit is quite alien to the Orthodox spirit. In principle it is the *Laós* and the clergy together who elect the bishops. In Cyprus this still happens : representatives democratically voted for in each village sit with the clergy to elect the new bishop—the same goes for the election of the archbishop. In Greece the people's part in the election of the bishops has been reduced to the crowd shouting "worthy, worthy" as the names of those who have been elected by the hierarchy are read out. This still gives the people a negative form of power, for it is not unknown for members of the crowd to shout "unworthy, unworthy" if they have something serious against one of the men elected. In 1961 the hierarchy elected Mgr Iakovos of Attica as Archbishop of Athens. Many shouts of "unworthy" were heard and about ten days after the election he was forced to resign because of the ferment in the press about his allegedly devious sexual behaviour. In other words, the *Laós* had used its power of veto to topple an archbishop.

The conception of the *Laós* as an active force to be respected in the life of the Church perhaps goes some way towards accounting for the absence of anti-cassock type anti-clericalism of the sort to be found in the West (see Chapter 2). In the intellectual sphere the clergy do not monopolize the teaching appointments in theological faculties and seminaries; they do not write all the books that appear on theological and religious subjects as they tend to do in the Catholic Church. Unlike their Catholic counterparts the Orthodox clergy have no monopoly in religious education and the preaching of sermons.

In Greece the complaint is rather that the priests do not, or through lack of education cannot, take their due part in the intellectual life of the Church. Out of the twenty or so university theology teachers in the faculties of Athens and Salonica only one is a priest. Consequently nearly all the serious theological works are produced by laymen. It is not unusual to find that the director of a seminary is a layman and the majority of the teachers are invariably lay people. Lay theologians fill nearly all the religious education posts in the secondary schools. If you stay till the end of Mass in any Athenian or provincial town parish on a Sunday you will more often than not hear a sermon preached by a layman. In Greek Orthodoxy it is the lay theologians who have taken over the thinking and teaching function that in the West has come to be the prerogative of the clergy. This is accepted by Greek priests, including the educated ones, who generally regard themselves as pastors and administrators. Even the bishops for the most part see themselves in this light and not as the intellectuals of Orthodoxy. In prodding bishops about their views on ecumenical matters one gets the impression that some of them really feel that these sort of problems are outside their ken and should be left to the lay university theology teachers.

Theology is a comparatively popular Arts subject among Greek students. As a result many more theology graduates are turned out than can possibly be given posts as teachers of religion in secondary schools. A few manage to get taken on as regular lay preachers in a provincial diocese, paid from the diocesan budget, and a few others get posts as secretaries in diocesan administration, but these are sideline jobs and hard to come by. Other solutions I have come across are theologians who opened private schools in places where there was no State school or even gave private language lessons if they happened to have studied abroad. However, the bulk of the theology graduates who have not yet been posted to State schools as teachers of religion just hang around and hope. There are about a thousand of them waiting and hoping. Those who took their degrees in 1960 should all have been posted by the end of 1966.

Greece has two theological faculties, Athens and Salonica. Athens is the older of the two, having been founded last century, while the Salonica school started only in 1942 (Salonica University itself only came into being in the 1920s). The teachers in the Salonica faculty are on the whole younger, many of them in their forties, than their Athenian colleagues and they seem more aware of what is going on abroad. In a four-year course the Athens faculty expects its students to study equally and without specialization a vast field of subjects which include: The Old Testament, the history of the New Testament, New Testament interpretation, Dogma, Patristics, Canon Law, Church history, Byzantine archaeology, Ethics, the history and philosophy of religion, pastoral theology, the liturgy, catechism and rhetoric. The average Athenian theology graduate comes away with an encyclopaedic acquaintance with all the branches of his study but with no specialized knowledge and often without the ability to think with the independence of mind that should be acquired in the course of a university training. The unfortunate Athenian student has little time to learn to think for himself since all his waking hours are taken up with memorizing facts and other people's opinions. Salonica used to have the same encyclopaedic curriculum, but since 1964 students have been able to choose one of three courses. People wishing to become secondary-school teachers take the purely theological course—they are thus dispensed from learning the techniques of the confessional and the intricacies of celebrating the liturgy. Students who want to become priests or who are already priests take the pastoral course and give the less essential theoretical lectures a miss. The third course is for theologians who will do ecclesiastical social work, in hospitals, etc. This is a new idea and no one is quite clear what sort of jobs graduates in this course are likely to find.

Until 1964 it was impossible to do a theological post-graduate course in Greece; people wishing to continue their studies had to go abroad. This partly explains why university teachers of theology are on the whole so keenly aware of Western theology, at least of Western works in their own particular field. Before the war most Greek post-graduate study was done in German Protestant universities. However, since 1945 an increasing number of theologians have been going to Catholic faculties in France, Germany and Switzerland. In 1964 the University of Salonica started offering two-year post-graduate courses to afford Greek students the opportunity of specializing without going abroad. In early 1965 there were five of these courses under way.

One has the impression that the teaching in Salonica is a good deal more personal than that in Athens. The department is smaller, the teachers younger and there is more of a feeling of the school being a corporate entity. Apart from eleven fully qualified lecturers the faculty also employs fifteen assistants. Each of these assistants is allocated to one of the full lecturers and acts as his right-hand man. The assistant supervises exams, is responsible for keeping order in the study rooms, helps the lecturer in his research and takes a limited number of classes himself. The assistants have nearly all done post-graduate courses abroad and many of them are preparing doctorate theses. The importance of the assistants is that, being mostly in their late twenties, they provide a human link between the lecturers and the students. Athens, in contrast to Salonica's fifteen, has only five assistants.

HOW ECUMENICALLY MINDED ARE THE THEOLOGIANS?

In any discussion of the prospects of reunion between the Catholic and Orthodox Churches the views of the theologians of Greece are of crucial importance. In terms of world Orthodoxy the Greeks and the Russians of the diaspora are the only important groups of Orthodox intellectuals who have freedom of contact with the West and its Churches. The largest Orthodox community, that in Russia, has been sealed off from effective contact with the West since 1917, and the Rumanians, Yugoslavs and Bulgarians have suffered the same isolation since 1945. The theologians in these countries rarely get the chance to travel outside the Iron Curtain bloc, the State makes it difficult for them to get new books from the West, and they have only limited freedom to publish their own real reactions to what is going on abroad.[1] In contrast to this the Greeks are completely free to travel and study abroad, to read foreign texts and to publish their own. As a result of the politically imposed situation in the countries of Orthodoxy's Slav cycle and in Rumania the main responsibility for understanding and expounding what is going on inside the Western Churches today lies with the theologians of the Greek cycle and those of the Russian diaspora.

Inside the Greek cycle the theologians of Greece itself have a dominating position. The Patriarchate of Constantinople has its own theological institute, but for all that the Patriarch borrowed

[1] See Appendix I for the situation of the Church in Bulgaria.

one of the Salonica theologians to be a lay member of his delegation to the Third Pan-Orthodox Conference that met in 1964 to
discuss how a dialogue with Rome might be opened. The other
two Greek Patriarchates in the Near East, Alexandria and Jerusalem, are numerically small communities and have depended
entirely on Greece's theologians to make up the non-episcopal side
of their delegations to the recent Pan-Orthodox Conferences (1961,
1963 and 1964). Most of the theologians of the autocephalous
Church of Cyprus have graduated from one or other of the two
universities in Greece.

As we have seen, in Greece itself the lay theologians are responsible for the lion's share of religious thinking and instruction.
They are the greatest single force influencing the attitude of the
people in ecumenical matters. The young theologian taking a
Sunday-school class has to decide whether he is going to teach his
pupils to look at the Western Churches in the way suggested by
the sour-minded compilers of the Apostolic Organization's catechism chapters on Protestantism and Catholicism (see Chapter 4),
or whether he is going to adopt a more ecumenical approach. His
own state of mind in turn depends on the attitudes of the people
who taught him at the university. The preacher preparing a
sermon at the time of the Pope–Patriarch meeting inevitably had
to make up his mind how he felt about it and convey these feelings
to his hearers. The issue was too important and aroused too much
discussion in Greece for it to be diplomatically sidestepped in
the pulpit. Lay theologians edit or write most of the articles in the
specialized religious press, which is read by the bishops, the clergy
and a few ecclesiastically-minded lay people. Through this medium
they have the possibility of forming clerical opinion on ecumenical
matters. Finally the university teachers of theology are frequently
given space in the national press to air their views on reunion
topics. They influence the readers of the newspapers directly by
their own writing and indirectly through the respect that journa-

sts have for their opinions. A non-theologian leader-writer told to
o a piece on something like the return of the skull of St Andrew
) Patras is very unlikely to fly in the face of a favourable con-
ensus of opinion among the experts, the university theologians.

A glance at the reaction of the university lecturers in theology
) the Pope–Patriarch meeting in January 1964 shows that as a
ody they are willing to consider the problems of *rapprochement*
rith Rome in a level-headed manner, quite unmoved by the fan-
tical outbursts of men like Archbishop Chrysostomos and the
roups round him. One of the very few to come out roundly
gainst the meeting was Professor[2] P. Panayiotakos, who wrote in
1e newspaper *Kathimerini*: "The Pope–Patriarch meeting was
ompletely useless and contrary to the canons of Holy Church. Its
:sult has been to strengthen the Latin view of the schism. . . .
'hat the two pontiffs in company with their retinues should have
rayed together shows overmuch eagerness and a want of reflection
1at is not without its dangers. . . ." The Professor went on to
:mind the Greeks what they had already suffered at the hands
f Rome in the past.

A moderately favourable reaction to the Jerusalem meeting, that
f Professor Kaloyirou,[3] was typical of the mainstream of opinion
mong the university theologians. He wrote that Constantinople
ras well aware of the difficulties of *rapprochement* with Rome
ut that she decided on the meeting out of an acute sense of her
:sponsibility towards Orthodoxy. Professor Kaloyirou then went
n to justify the negative stand of the Church of Greece by saying
1at she was still hyper-conscious of the wrongs done to her by the
:atholics in the past, "wrongs that continue in the form of

[2] All lecturers in Greek universities have the title "*Kathigitis*". Since
ecturer" and "teacher" in English cannot be used as titles qualifying a
ame, out of considerations of courtesy I have opted for the title "professor"
hen referring to university theology teachers. This does not imply head-
ip of a faculty.
[3] In the newspaper *Ethnos*, 4 Jan. 1964.

Uniatism which is at work with full freedom in the heart of Greece . . .". About the meeting of the two Pontiffs he showed a guarded optimism : "We hope this meeting will bear fruit in the future and that it will be followed by other meetings between Orthodoxy and Western Catholicism, which [the latter] undoubtedly has greater influence and authority in the contemporary world than any other power or institution. . . ."

Professor Christos wrote on a somewhat warmer note :[4] "Careful preparation will be necessary on both sides if the action of the two leaders in meeting each other is not to prove vain. But the very fact that the dialogue should have been begun by the meeting of the two leaders is the happiest of prologues and cannot be left without a follow-up. . . ." Of the Pope Professor Christos wrote : "Mankind has discovered in Pope Paul VI a quite different Pope from what they had imagined and from the Popes of history. Men have come to recognize a Pope full of spiritual life and humility who had no hesitation in showing his feelings of love by kissing the Patriarch, his eyes full of tears produced by the emotion of the moment. . . . Vatican protocol and the Swiss Guard were no longer in evidence. . . ."

In an interview with the paper *Ethnos* (21 January 1964) M. Keramidas, President of the Association of Lay Theologians, said of the meeting : "Without any hesitation whatsoever I can say I think the meeting between the heads of the two Churches will certainly turn out to have been very useful . . . history will recognize the importance of the Ecumenical Patriarch's noble gesture. . . ."

To the Western reader favourable reaction to the Jerusalem meeting of the sort quoted above may seem entirely natural and to be expected. However, in the Greek atmosphere in which especially in ecclesiastical circles, suspicion and even hatred of the Papacy has been dominant for centuries, the theologians' on the

[4] In the newspaper *Acropolis*, 12 Jan. 1964.

whole favourable reaction to the meeting of the two leaders is a great ecumenical step forward.

Compared to the bishops and the clergy the lay theologians are comparatively well informed on what is going on in the ecumenical sphere abroad. However, despite the fact that the Athens and Salonica faculties are sent the full texts of the Vatican Council decisions, when I interviewed some of the teachers in January 1965 many of them had clearly not got round to reading the relevant matter on the third session which had ended nearly two months before. The ones who had were those with a specialized interest in one particular text—a teacher of Church history, for example, was aware of the contents of the Constitution on the Church. On the whole the Salonica staff seemed more ecumenically aware than their Athenian colleagues. This was particularly so among such teachers as had been abroad recently and seen with their own eyes what the *aggiornamento* was beginning to mean on a practical level inside Catholicism. Mr Tsananas, a Salonica assistant lecturer who recently spent three years at the Catholic University of Münster, was fully alive to the intense struggle inside Catholicism between the progressive and the conservative wings. In the light of this struggle he saw the *De Ecclesia* decree as being still unsatisfactory to an Orthodox but certainly as much as he had ever hoped could be achieved by the Catholic Church at this stage. He took the realistic view that it is much easier for the Orthodox to have a fruitful dialogue with the Catholics than with the Protestants because in the former case the thorniest difficulties are ecclesiological and not dogmatic; they are consequently less basic.

One of the things that strikes one when thumbing through the things the Greek theologians have written about ecumenical matters over the last few years is that they are always reacting to things said or done by the other side and rarely thinking and proposing positively themselves. This is strange at a time when two Rhodes (Pan-Orthodox) Conferences have expressed a desire to start a dialogue with Rome. A typical example of this passive attitude to ecumenical matters was an article in *Ekklisia* (1 February 1965) by Professor Karmiris of Athens University who is ecumenically well informed without being at all enthusiastic. He suggested that the fourth session of the Vatican Council should "neutralize and dispel" the unfavourable impression made on the Orthodox by the emphasis in the Pope's speeches on his absolute primacy and of the return of the Orthodox to the Roman fold, by the Eastern Churches decree and by other things said in and acted on by the Council in its first three sessions. The Professor continued : "These and other similar things, seen in the light of our bitter historical experience of the Roman Church, inclined the delegates at the third Pan-Orthodox Conference to feel that the time was not yet ripe for the opening of an Orthodox-Catholic dialogue."

There are two university theologians in Greece today who stand out from the rest as being positively concerned with the *rapprochement* of the Catholic and Orthodox Churches. Their approach is creative in that they feel that they themselves can do something, however small, to help prepare the climate in Greece for ecumenical developments in the future. The younger of the two, in his forties, is Professor Agouridis of Salonica. He feels that the most important thing he can do is to try to "humanize" the atmosphere in which he lives. He sees four ways of doing this : firstly by writing articles that praise sensible ecumenical developments and deplore the rantings of the local fanatics. For instance, he wrote an article in the newspaper *Kathimerini* (15 December 1964) deploring the decision of the third Pan-Orthodox Conference to put off the dialogue with Rome until at least after the end of the Vatican Council. He also deplored the Greek hierarchy's expression of satisfaction with the results of the conference.

A second way of humanizing the atmosphere is by trying to produce a more ecumenical climate of opinion among the theology students. He told me that most of them were open to progressive ideas, except for a few reactionary groups. He suggested that the students affiliated to *Sotir* and *Zoi* without being fanatical are "ecumenically slow". One way of showing the students what Catholicism is about is by bringing eminent Catholics to lecture to the faculty. The speakers that go down best are patristic experts like Fr Daniélou who came two or three years ago and spoke to packed audiences. Professor Agouridis's third objective is to have some ecumenical teaching introduced into the books used for religious education in secondary schools. He is pressing the Ministry of Education and Religion to include a short ecumenical section in the new text-books now in preparation. His final way of trying to humanize the atmosphere was the formation in 1963 of a tiny ecumenical discussion group, not unlike the one in Athens (see Chapter 2). Every three weeks a dozen theologians, Orthodox, Catholic, an Evangelical and a Quaker, meet and discuss a non-controversial subject such as "The relation of the individual to the person of Christ" or "How do you visualize the Kingdom of God?" The group meets in a private house and has not so far organized any public gatherings.

Professor Agouridis is an encouraging feature on the Greek theological landscape not only on account of the ecumenical action he undertakes but also because of the realistic attitudes which underlie that action. He told me he holds the Orthodox faith to be the true one, but that he is far from thinking that its present-day form is perfect. To him the basis of any real ecumenism is repentance on both sides and this inevitably implies withdrawal by both the Orthodox and the Catholics from certain stands which have been maintained up till now.

The second pre-eminently ecumenically-minded theologian in Greece is Professor Hamilcar Alivizatos, formerly a teacher in Athens University and now the State's representative in the Holy Synod. In body he is an old man but in mind he conserves the

E

vigour of a man half his age. Underlying and presupposing Professor Alivizatos's ecumenical outlook is a full grasp of the facts, combined with insight. He is fully informed about all the latest developments in the West (both Catholic and Protestant) and he has the insight, gained by frequent contact with the West, necessary to interpret these developments with a sharp lucidity lacking in many of his colleagues. For all his appreciation of the West Professor Alivizatos remains profoundly Orthodox in his manner of thinking and his appraisals. His more fanatical opponents call him a "Protestant" because of his long association with the World Council of Churches and his habit of travelling in Northern European countries. If he is a "Protestant" his comments on Vatican II (see below) show him to be a very ecumenically-minded one! The Professor's attitude to the work of the Vatican Council has been consistently positive and even when things have happened in Rome that could please no Orthodox he has always tried to see them and interpret them in their true context inside Catholicism. He has repeatedly condemned the negative and defensive reaction of the Greek Church to developments abroad. What follows are summaries of some of Professor Alivizatos's articles in the newspaper *Vima* published since the start of the Council.

On 13 March 1963 (after the first session) he wrote that the non-participation of observers from the Greek Church was a "historic mistake" which must not be repeated at the second session of the Council (it was). He warmly praised the welcome and working facilities extended to the non-Catholic observers at the Council. Of particular note were the ease of access the observers had to the person of Pope John and the way they were invited to comment on the Council's work. The Professor attributed the non-participation of Greek observers to "our own ignorance, disorder and inconsistency".

At the time of the second session Professor Alivizatos described[5]

[5] In *Vima* of 27 and 30 Oct. 1963.

the Council as a "peaceful revolution" in the Catholic Church which would clear the way for a real dialogue between Rome and the other Christian Churches. He highlighted nine features of the Council that substantially reduce the gap between the Catholic and Orthodox Churches :

(1) The opportunity for observers from Churches formerly regarded by Rome as heretical or schismatic to witness personally the most secret deliberations of the Catholic Church.

(2) The revision of the theological basis of the Catholic Church's nature and substance. The Professor wrote : "The emphasis laid by the Church on the mystical body of Christ according to St Paul (Ephesians 4. 1-6) with its inevitable repercussions in Church organization creates a favourable climate and prepares the ground for agreement among all Christians. . . ."

(3) The effort to correct "the mistake made by the First Vatican Council" with regard to Papal infallibility and primacy by stressing the collective authority of the college of bishops as successors to the Apostles. This effort opens the door to a *rapprochement* with the Orthodox concept of the democratic nature of Church authority.

(4) Pope Paul's call for reform of the Curia, which stands in reactionary opposition to the "healthy-minded clergy of the Catholic Church".

(5) The discussion by the Council of the possible ordination of married deacons.

(6) The use of national languages in the Mass and in the liturgy in place of Latin's former monopoly. (The Orthodox missionary has always translated the liturgy into the language of the particular nation or tribe to be evangelized.)

(7) The possibility of a partial return to communion in both kinds as instituted by Christ.

(8) Cardinal Lercaro of Bologna's suggestion that the Church concern herself more with the problems of contemporary society,

especially poverty, and that she shed her appearance of luxury (for example, the wealth of the Princes of the Church). Professor Alivizatos sees this as a desire to return to the simplicity of the early Church.

(9) The likely decision to rehabilitate the lay element in Church life on the basis of the sacraments of baptism and confirmation that each layman has received. Such a decision would draw the Catholic Church much closer to Orthodoxy and Protestantism.

Professor Alivizatos again roundly condemned the Church of Greece for missing the opportunity of witnessing the great revolution in the Catholic Church by sending observers. He wrote : "Our policy is modelled on the behaviour of Lot's wife, who instead of hastening forward to her salvation kept on looking back."

A clear idea can be had of the contrast between Alivizatos' constructive, positive ecumenism and the paler, more negative approach of most of his colleagues if one compares reactions to the Pope–Patriarch meeting quoted earlier in this chapter to what he wrote in Vima on 17, 19 and 20 May 1964. The Professor said the Holy Land meeting had broken the ice of nine centuries and ushered in a new historical period in the relations between Catholicism and Orthodoxy. The next step is a dialogue between the two Churches which must first and foremost be one "of love and true peace. The centuries and their harsh happenings have left us with indifference, ignorance, suspicion, enmity, hate, crimes and fanaticism. The dialogue of love must look this legacy in the face and completely wipe it away." While the spirit of the dialogue must be one of love its subject-matter must be theological. Orthodoxy must prepare her positions and pick her top experts in each branch of theology that is to be thrashed out in discussion with the Catholics. There must be no use of second- or third-class theological ammunition in such a dialogue : "there would be no room for argument drawn from the goings on of the Middle Ages which were clearly as passionate as they were puerile".

At various points in his three articles Professor Alivizatos stressed the absolute necessity for full preparation on both sides before any theological dialogue be started. He wrote that "although our present-day Orthodoxy is not fully prepared and armed to face the rich and fully mobilized theology of the West" he has faith in the help and inspiration of God and in the favourable disposition of both sides. "The dialogue must be a dialogue of real, and not merely verbal or rhetorical repentance and recognition of the mistakes made by both sides. . . . No harm can come from our freely and sincerely admitting that such and such a pope, patriarch or emperor committed errors, because they were unable to escape from the bitter medieval atmosphere in which they lived and had to act." The dialogue must take place on a truly equal footing. According to Professor Alivizatos this means that one section of the Christian Church has the democratic right to examine and criticize other sections of the Church, without this right giving rise to pretensions of superiority—the examination should be conducted as a brotherly duty. Finally the Professor warned that statements by the Pope stressing his own infallibility can only make difficulties for the Eastern Churches, difficulties of a psychological rather than theological order.

The basis of Alivizatos's ecumenism is a charity that seeks to understand and explain rather than condemn positions taken up by the "other side" that seem to put obstacles in the way of *rapprochement*. He shares the disappointment of most Orthodox theologians over many of the happenings in the third session. Though he had not expected *De Ecclesia* radically to alter Catholic ecclesiology he told me he feels that the decree as it stands goes out of its way to emphasize the Pope's "superior prestige and supreme authority" in relation to the college of bishops. A council interested in reconciling other Christians might have laid less stress on the question of papal power. Though he shares the other theologians' disappointment, he is not content to share their passive "let's wait and see what happens next" attitude. He went on to tell me (in an interview in spring 1965) that it is now clear that the Western Church cannot abandon her centralized system which depends on papal primacy of power as well as of honour. Nor can the Eastern Church abandon her democratic form of government and accept the system of papal rule in her sector. A fruitful line of discussion in future Orthodox–Catholic dialogue would be exploration of the idea of "co-existence" which was the working *status quo* in the final two or three centuries preceding the 1054 schism. In those centuries the Pope was building up his prerogatives and powers in the West, but he did not interfere in the running of the Eastern half of Christendom. In like manner the East did not interfere in the Western Church's business. Despite the fact that decade by decade the differences between East and West were increasing the Easterner could receive all the seven sacraments if he happened to be in Rome as could the Westerner in Constantinople. The Church was fundamentally and sacramentally one despite growing organizational and temperamental differences between West and East. The Professor told me that if it were possible to restore full *communicatio in sacris*, as the Catholic Church has now allowed in cases of need, we would be back to the *status quo* before the schism. East and West would retain their respective systems of government but the *Church* would be sacramentally one.

The sensibleness of the tone and the arguments used by the lay theologians in their public exposition (through the newspapers) of ecumenical matters contrasts sharply with the hysteria of the anti-ecumenical fringe led by Archbishop Chrysostomos, Abbot Vasilo-poulos and Fr Kandiotis. That the newspapers and educated lay people generally tend to be mildly favourable to the *rapprochement* of the Churches (see Chapter 2) shows that in this sector of society at least reason has triumphed over the inherited fear and suspicion that the Greeks have in the past nurtured towards Rome. If this has happened it is largely to the credit of the lay theologians.

7
religious nationalism
and a broader view

Night was falling as the "Republican" (leftist) army entered the village. The mayor and the garde-champêtre were seized and taken out of the village to be executed. The Communists sent fifteen other villagers with them. An hour later someone came back for a mattock and a spade. In the meantime the mayor's arms and legs had been hacked off and the garde-champêtre had been tortured to death.

Just after midnight they came for Papa Thanasis. The poor man knew what was coming to him. He put on his vestments and set off to face his calvary, accompanied by an escort.

The road up to the place of death was steep and it took them an hour to get there. All along the way the bandits cursed and scoffed at him. When the priest finally reached the place he found the fifteen villagers lined up in a row with opposite them his executioners. One man stood apart from both groups, the bandit Bousgos, a native of the village.

Papa Thanasis was not even given time to regain his breath. They tied him to a fir tree and Bousgos drove his bayonet into the priest's left shoulder. The blade went right through. The "Republican hero" left the bayonet where it was for the time it took him to smoke a cigarette.

When he had finished his smoke Bousgos tore the bayonet out and drove it into the other shoulder. Then he and his companions again started mocking the crucified man. After beating the priest about the stomach Bousgos finished him off with a bayonet thrust to the head.[1]

Papa Thanasis was only one of nearly 400 Greek priests murdered between 1941 and 1950. Some fell victim to the Bulgarians

[1] An extract from a letter to the newspaper *Embros* reprinted in a Greek Foreign Office propaganda pamphlet (1947).

and Germans who occupied Greece from 1941 to 1944 while others, like Papa Thanasis, were killed in a variety of ways, including crucifixion, by the Greek leftists in the 1946–49 civil war. Though a number of these priests were murdered in settlement of personal scores, the majority died for their faith and their nation in the sense that they were the local symbols of both faith and nation. There is nothing new or strange, in terms of Greek history since the fall of Byzantium (1453), in the priest standing as the symbol of both faith and nation.

Under Byzantium the temporal power of the Emperor and the spiritual power of the Patriarch of Constantinople were in theory separate spheres, though the emperor in fact often intervened in the affairs of the Church. With the conquest of the Empire by the Muslim Turks the role of the Church was radically altered. The Turks did not see their new empire as consisting of various linguistic and ethnic groups (Greeks, Slavs, etc.) but as consisting of believers and non-believers. The Ottoman Empire's non-believers were governed in three main millets, or religious communities, the Orthodox Christians, the Armenian Christians and the Jews. The millets were governed through their separate hierarchies. In this way the Patriarch of Constantinople became responsible to the Sultan for the administration of all the latter's Orthodox subjects, irrespective of their language, geographical location or ethnic group. It was the Patriarch through the bishops who collected certain dues imposed on the Christians and he would intercede with the Sultan if injustice were done to members of his millet. In other words, the Orthodox Church was forced to become the immediate temporal authority over the Christians as well as being their spiritual guide. The hierarchy did not grab this power, it was imposed on them by the Turkish system.

When the wind of revolution began to blow among the Sultan's Greek subjects in the early nineteenth century the hierarchy and clergy were intimately involved. It was they who, by their teach-

ng and through the liturgy, had helped keep the language and
traditions of Byzantium alive during four centuries of foreign
domination. They were both the link with what the Greeks saw
as the glorious past and the effective leaders of the day. Despite the
higher clergy's vested interest in the Ottoman *status quo* and suspicion of some of the secular leaders, the 1821 revolution was proclaimed from the monastery of Agia Lavra in the Peloponnese by
the Bishop of Patras, Germanos. The banner of the revolution was
the curtain of the main door into the sanctuary of Patras Cathedral
which Germanos gave the nationalist leaders to cut short bickering
about whose family flag to adopt. While Germanos played the part
of an active Ethnarch in the revolution, Patriarch Gregory V of
Constantinople baptized it with his blood. On hearing of the up-
rising the Sultan had him hanged from the lintel of the main gate
into the Patriarchal palace, the Phanar—the hanging took place
at the end of the Easter Sunday Mass in 1821. The Greeks of the
Peloponnese accepted Germanos as their symbolic leader in starting the revolt and the Sultan held the Patriarch responsible for the
doings of the Orthodox Christians of the Empire. The circumstances of Turkish rule and the 1821 revolution made it inevitable
that the Greek clergy should become the focus of religious and
national loyalty in the new Greek State.

The rebellion of the other Orthodox peoples of the Ottoman
Empire later in the nineteenth century shared many of the religio-
nationalistic characteristics of the Greek prototype. One of the first
things the new States did was to set up their own national
Churches independent of the administrative jurisdiction of the
Greek Patriarchate of Constantinople. The new Churches then
speedily rid their hierarchies of the Greek element that under
Turkish rule had often been predominant. In a country like Bulgaria there was almost as much dislike of Greek religious hege-
mony as hate of Turkish political domination. In fact ecclesiastical
independence from the Patriarchate was achieved eight years

before statehood, 1870 and 1878 respectively. This antipathy for th
Greeks went right back to the days when one of Byzantium's mai
aims had been the absorption of the Bulgarian kingdom into th
Empire. The Bulgars had not and still today have not forgotte
that one of the Byzantine emperors bears the proud title of Basi
the Bulgar-slayer. As far as Orthodoxy is concerned the fruit o
the nineteenth-century Balkan revolutions is that the Patriarchat
of Constantinople, which under the Byzantine and Ottoman ré
gimes was a united whole, has been broken up into a number o
small, autocephalous and nationalistically inspired Churches be
tween which little contact has been possible owing to the ethni
and territorial antagonisms of their respective States. The stronges
antagonism has been that between the Greeks and the Slavs
Contact between the Greek and Slav Churches which before 194
was slight has since been further hampered by the falling of th
Iron Curtain. The Greco-Bulgarian frontier, for instance, onl
opened to ordinary travellers in late 1964.

The nationalism of the modern Greek is founded on two over
lapping ideals, that of the *Patrida* (Mother-land) and that of th
Ethnos (race or nation). The *Patrida* ideal involves the defence o
territory that Greece already possesses (in other words, patriotism)
while the *Ethnos* ideal demands the acquisition of new territor
that the Greeks feel to be rightly theirs. It was the *Patrida* idea
that inspired the determined Greek repulse of Mussolini's invasio
from Albania in 1940. It was the *Ethnos* ideal that led to th
disastrous Asia Minor campaign in the early 1920s and which toda
keeps the feeling that Cyprus should be united to Greece at red
hot temperature. Both the *Patrida* and *Ethnos* ideals are inextric
ably bound up with religious feeling.

An excellent example of how unravellable are the concepts o
Patrida and faith to the Greek way of thinking comes in th
chapter on "No" Day in one of the Apostolic Organization'
catechism books for working youth. ("No" Day was 28 Octobe

1940 when Prime Minister Metaxas refused to capitulate before Mussolini's divisions massed on the Albanian frontier.) The first interesting thing is that the chapter on "No" Day is one of a series on religious feastdays, the implication being that "No" Day is a religious feastday, rather as if the Church of England were to list the anniversary of Dunkirk as a feast in the religious calendar along with St George's Day and Christmas. The writer of the chapter states that the repulse of the Italians was another of those victories in which "faith together with love of country brought about the salvation of our Nation". Other similar victories he quotes are Constantine's triumph over Maxentius, the repulse of the Arabs from Constantinople and the 1821 revolution. He goes on : "The faith of the Greek people was the belief in one God, all-powerful, all-just and all-strong, who can overthrow the mighty and give victory to the weak. So with this faith in the all-powerful and all-just God the Greek people went into the fight." The writer then quotes letters written by soldiers on the front which further demonstrate the identification of the two loyalties of faith and country : "It is not the danger we are in that makes us have this faith. No, it is the miracles we have seen with our own eyes, it is the victories that we have won through the power of God. These have obliged us, forced us, to believe in God who loves Greece." Another letter tells how the soldiers treat their prisoners in a manner befitting Christians and Greeks : "You cannot be a Christian, believing in and asking for the help of God, if you do not help the enemy who has fallen into your hands. You cannot be a Greek if you do not show nobility."

The best current example of the power of the *Ethnos* ideal is over the Cyprus struggle for reunion with Greece. In this affair the clergy of both Greece and the island have taken on once again the ethnarchic role which was theirs in 1821. In 1964 a Greek paper carried a picture of three Cypriot priests conducting an outdoor service—on the platform next to the temporary altar were three rifles, with fixed bayonets, propped up in the form of a tripod. The caption above the picture ran : "Like 1821, Gospel and guns together." The caption underneath read : "The English, who published this photograph in one of their papers, write : 'Guns where the Gospel should be.' The truth is otherwise; the rifles are there to protect the Gospel from profanation by the unbelievers, urged on by their protectors, the English." Not only is there nothing strange to the Greek mind about an archbishop leading a revolt, but if he shunned this duty he would be condemned. In times of need the Church and the nation become one and the pulpit is thought to be a legitimate ethnic platform. Preaching in Alexandria after the Turkish bombing of Kokkina in 1964, Archbishop Makarios thought a church the fit theatre for these words : "We will not surrender. We have decided to fight for honour and to die but not let the Barbarians pass. . . . We have suffered from pressure, blackmail and from barbaric and bestial bombings. . . ." There are few Greeks who would condemn the use of the pulpit for the expression of this sort of political reaction. To the Greeks Makarios's struggle is not a political one though the means may sometimes be political; it is an ethnic one and thus holy and above politics. On several occasions in the past few years the bishops of Greece have ordered preachers to devote the Sunday sermon to harangues on Cyprus. Seminary students are encouraged to join student demonstrations on Cyprus and on some occasions have led marches bearing Eoka placards. Greek attitudes have indeed changed since the time when the highly cultured Byzantine clergy were amazed at the sight of Frankish baron-bishops swinging their maces and battle-axes below the walls of Constantinople. The Byzantines were at a loss to understand how ministers of the Word of peace could at the same time be war leaders.

One of the unfortunate results of the Greek ethnic-religious ideal is a chauvinistic attitude to other Orthodox peoples and to the West. Though this chauvinistic attitude underlies much of

Greek thinking, it is most easily illustrated from its most extreme manifestation which occurs in monastic communities. Abbot Vasilopoulos of the Petraki monastery (see Chapter 5) told me without a blush that he sees the Greeks as the second chosen people. According to his theory, after Christ's crucifixion they took over this role in the world from the Jews who had rendered themselves unworthy of it. To support the theory he pointed out that the Gospels (three of them) were written in Greek and that all the great dogmatically formative Councils of the Church were the work of the Greeks. In Vasilopoulos's notion that the Greeks are "the chosen people" one finds a total identification of the religion with the *Patrida* and *Ethnos*.

Fascinating extremes of Greek historical chauvinism are to be found on Mount Athos. After some forty conversations with monks on the Mountain one can piece together a potted history of Greece along these lines : When you in the West were still savages we had great thinkers, Aristotle, Plato . . . whom have you to compare with them? At the time of Alexander the Great the Greeks ruled the world. The Roman Empire is then passed over in discreet silence. History re-starts with Constantine and the erection of Christianity into the official religion of the Empire. It was the Greek Fathers who evolved Christian theology. It was the Greek missionaries who brought Christianity to the Balkan Slavs and the Russians. In 1054 Rome deviated from the path of true Christianity and the Reformation was a direct result of, and punishment for this sad mistake. With the fall of Constantinople civilization was well-nigh extinguished, after the great pan-ethnic Christian State of Byzantium had been weakened by the attacks of the Pope-inspired crusaders. Greek scholars fled to the West which consequently emerged from the Dark Ages while we Greeks languished under the Turkish yoke. In 1821 came the glorious resurrection of the Greek people. Since then we have not quite caught up with the West, but 400 years of slavery and enforced backwardness is a long

time to have to catch up on. We hate the Turks for having op-
pressed us and the foreigners (the West) for preventing us from
expanding and regaining our former greatness. After the Asia
Minor campaign the Allies refused to let us keep our capital, Constantinople, and after World War II they would not give us back
Northern Epirus (today Southern Albania). The English have
tricked us cunningly over Cyprus which is an integral part of
Greece. They are afraid of our becoming a great power—look how
we rolled back the Italians in Albania. And so it goes on.

In one form or another this view of history is to be heard in
innumerable coffee-shop conversations in a hundred Greek villages, though in a less worked out form than that found on Athos.
Just as Abbot Vasilopoulos's view that the Greeks are the "chosen
people" does not facilitate friendly contact with the non-Greek
Orthodox, the Athonite and popular view of Greek history outlined above does not predispose uneducated Greek people to
approval of ecumenical contact with the West.

One of the main presuppositions of an Orthodox–Catholic
dialogue is that the partners in the dialogue should be the one
Orthodox Church and the one Catholic Church rather than the
many Orthodox Churches and the one Catholic Church. If Orthodoxy is to face Catholicism as a united whole the separate Orthodox
Churches must get to know one another again and enter into
regular contact. The problem of getting to know the sister
Churches is one that is beginning to worry certain young theologians in Greece. A number of serious attempts are being made
by these theologians to break down the barriers of ignorance and
nationalism that divide Orthodoxy.

The first problem is that of language. The normal foreign languages among Greek theologians are German, French and English. It is rare to find a Greek theologian with a grasp of Russian,
Rumanian or Bulgarian. This means that it is impossible for the
Greeks to follow what their fellow Orthodox theologians are

writing in these countries and impossible for them to communicate directly with them when they meet them, unless through a Western language foreign to both parties. In Bulgaria, for example, the ignorance of Greek in ecclesiastical circles is as widespread as the ignorance of Bulgarian in similar circles in Greece. To my knowledge there is only one competent Greek speaker among the Bulgarian theologians. An attempt to break down the language barrier from the Greek side is being made by the Institute of Macedonian Studies in Salonica. Its director, a lay theologian called Mr Tachiaos, runs a course for people in Salonica wishing to learn Russian or Bulgarian. Nearly half of the assistants in the Salonica theology department are at present learning Russian. (A knowledge of Russian affords contact with all educated people in the Orthodox Iron Curtain countries since it is today the first foreign language taught in their schools and since Russian influence in these countries long pre-dated the mushrooming of People's Republics.)

After the language problem, one of the most serious barriers to Orthodox inter-communication is that the theologians in one country have little idea what those in another are writing, even supposing they could read it. In order to remedy this situation a group of young Greek theologians have decided to set up a centre for co-ordinating Orthodox theological studies. The first aim of the centre, called *The Wisdom of God* (*I tou Theou Sophia*), is to produce a complete bibliography to cover all the questions that the first Pan-Orthodox Conference decided should be on the agenda of the future Pan-Orthodox pro-synod. (The pro-synod is looked forward to as a sort of *aggiornamento* council for Orthodoxy.) The bibliography is to be drawn up with the help of theologians from Orthodox communities all over the world. When it has collected the necessary money the *Wisdom of God* centre aims to build up an inter-Orthodoxy library where researchers will be able to find collected in one place "the immense treasures of

Orthodoxy that are scattered here and there in studies and periodicals".[2] Plans for the future include the setting up of an archive of photographs, films and records of the Orthodox liturgy from all over the world, the teaching of the languages of other Orthodox countries and the setting up of a special office for ecumenical relations. The young theologians behind the *Wisdom of God* centre are ecumenically minded in a thoroughly systematic way. They feel that the first job is to get to know their Orthodox brothers and then, together with them, to turn outwards towards the West. They take great interest in what has been happening at the Vatican Council and one of them went to Rome for three weeks during the third session.

The centre's most solid accomplishment to date is the production of an inter-Orthodox quarterly, *Orthodox Presence*. The whole of the first number (autumn 1964) was devoted to the subject of inter-Orthodox unity and most of the second (spring 1965) to the third Pan-Orthodox Conference. The articles were written by contributors from all over the Orthodox world and the first number included two articles by non-Orthodox theologians, one a French Catholic and the other a Swedish Protestant. Though the first two numbers came out only in Greek it is hoped that at some time in the future it will be possible to produce Greek, Russian and French editions.

Mr Tachiaos's Slav language courses in Salonica and the *Wisdom of God* centre in Athens aim at better communication between the theologians in the various Orthodox countries. Both efforts are too specialized to be likely to have much immediate effect on the general educated public in Greece. In recent years, however, the *Zoi* Brotherhood has been becoming more and more aware of the need to break away from the traditional, narrow, nationalistic way of looking at Orthodoxy and, as we saw in

[2] A quotation from the centre's periodical *Orthodox Presence* (*Orthodóxos Parousía*).

Chapter 4, they have considerable influence among middle-class Greek people. The journal of their Professional People's Association has started publishing articles by foreign Orthodox contributors and the *Zoi* magazine two years ago ran a series of articles on the state of the Russian Orthodox Church. In 1964 the Brotherhood published in book form a report in English on the state of all the Orthodox communities in the world. The chapter on each community was written by a locally resident theologian, or a native of the country in exile. Fr Mastroyiannopoulos, the superior of the *Zoi* Brotherhood, writing in the Professional People's journal *Aktines* in 1964, did not mince his words in condemning the chauvinistic nationalism that has up till now impeded contact between the Orthodox of different countries. He wrote :

> We bear the guilt for the scandal of the lack of communication and lack of community of spirit among the Orthodox Churches. Today when all men are uniting, we do not unite. We who are the universal Church do not live this reality and do not witness to it. . . . There is no worse scandal than that of divided Orthodoxy. Let us understand this clearly and repent. It is never too late. Let us humbly take our part in the great work of inter-Orthodox *rapprochement* in a spirit of faith, hope and love. Let us play our part in knocking down the walls of chauvinism, ethnicism, isolationism and autocephalism. Let us become aware of and declare the fact that we are not alone and that we cannot live alone. . . .

The more Orthodoxy, and Greek Orthodoxy in particular, is able to rid itself of its chauvinism, ethnicism, isolationism and autocephalism, the more hope there will be of a positive Orthodox–Catholic dialogue.

Another group determined to break down Greek isolationism inside Orthodoxy is the *Porefthentes* missionary committee. This started in 1959 as an offshoot of the International Organization of Orthodox Youth, *Syndesmos*, and has since started publishing its own magazine (circulation in 1965 about 2,500). The aims of the

committee are to reanimate the missionary conscience in the Orthodox Church, study the practical and theoretical needs of the
missions, help small missionary Churches and prepare the first
Greek missionary team. Up to date its main practical work has
been collection of money for the embryo Orthodox Churches in
Kenya, Uganda and Tanzania and help given to some thirty
East African students who have come to study in Greece. The
leader of this missionary movement, Fr Yannoulatos, was formerly a monk in the *Zoi* Brotherhood but left them because of
their exclusive concentration on the home mission. To his way of
thinking it is impossible to work for the good of the Greek
Church alone. Fr Yannoulatos wrote : [3]

"I believe in the one, holy, catholic and apostolic Church,' we
repeat unceasingly in almost every single service of worship. This is
the assurance which the bishops, before their consecration, must give
publicly. How then is it possible for the faithful and particularly for
the clergyman to think, to judge or to decide in terms of "his own"
province alone, "his own" needs only? The whole perspective of
the *one* Church and its total needs is what should always be before
our eyes, what should become the main characteristic of our yearnings
and actions at all times. Selfish absorption in "our own" needs and
indifference towards those of others denote that our belief in *one*
Church is reduced to a mere verbal formula. Whenever we say "our
Church", if we sincerely want to live as Orthodox, we are called to
think in terms of the Church that extends "from end to end of
the universe", as we say in the offering of the Holy Eucharist (liturgy
of St Basil the Great). There are not various Orthodox Churches,
such as the Church of Greece, the Church of Russia, the Church of
Rumania, of Japan, of Uganda and so on, but *one* Orthodox Church
"which is in Greece, in Russia, in Rumania, in Uganda, etc."

Fr Yannoulatos told me he feels that the process of involvement
in the foreign missions will draw the Greeks out of their nationalistic shell and make them first of all become aware of their fellow

[3] In the *St Vladimir Seminary Quarterly*, vol. 8, 3.

Orthodox in other countries. This in its turn will lead to a greater readiness for ecumenical encounter with the Christians of other Churches.

Certain of the younger generation of theologians in Greece are beginning to realize and react against the religious harmfulness of the heritage of ecclesiastical nationalism handed down from the time of the 1821 revolution and subsequent wars of liberation. They are determined to broaden their countrymen's attitude to Orthodoxy and show them that their religion's glory lies first and foremost in its claim to universality and not in the fact that it happens to be the religion of Greece. They will have a hard job of it.

8
the phanar[1] and world orthodoxy

THE PATRIARCHATE of Constantinople has three distinct spheres of responsibility. The Patriarch is firstly bishop of the Greeks in Turkey (the only Greeks left in any numbers in Turkey live in Istanbul and on the islands of Imbros and Tenedos); secondly he has under his direct jurisdiction the monasteries of Athos, and two and a half million Orthodox in Crete, Rhodes, Western Europe, Australia and America (in the U.S., apart from the Greek Orthodox, certain Slav diaspora communities come under Constantinople); thirdly the Patriarch of Constantinople is the Ecumenical Patriarch, the first among equals of the heads of the autocephalous Orthodox Churches.

Let us first consider the Patriarch in his capacity as bishop of the Greeks in Turkey. As mentioned in the last chapter, the Patriarch under the Ottoman Empire (1453–1918) was held responsible for the temporal administration of all the Orthodox within Ottoman territory. With the foundation of the secular State in Turkey in the 1920s all this changed, at least from the official Turkish side. Turkey's Orthodox subjects were no longer ruled through their religious hierarchy—the majority of them took Turkish nationality and stood before the law like any other Turkish citizens. Those with Greek nationality were granted residence permits as foreigners. Official Turkey regards the Patriarch as bishop of the "Orthodox Turks",[2] which explains the rule that the bishop

[1] The Phanar is the Ecumenical Patriarch of Constantinople's residence in Istanbul. Constantinople is the Byzantine name for the city the Turks call Istanbul.
[2] The term "Orthodox Turks" does not here refer to Papa Effendim's "Orthodox Turkish Church", with the liturgy in Turkish, that was started

148

elected Patriarch must have Turkish nationality.[3] Other regulations imposed on the Orthodox Church in Istanbul emphasize the official Turkish view that the Patriarchate is mainly there to minister to the "Turkish" Orthodox. For example, the Patriarchate's theological institute at Halki may take only a limited percentage of students (35 per cent of total intake) with nationalities other than Turkish. All the students in the school must know Turkish, and if they don't, they must learn it. If a foreign student fails his exam in Turkish he risks not getting an extension of his residence permit. One of the ideas behind these regulations is that boys trained in the school are meant to become priests ministering to the local Orthodox population—in fact this is not the case since Halki has students from Greece and many other parts of the Orthodox world who return home after graduating. It is Halki's international character that Turkey wants to restrict by limiting the number of foreign entrants.

The present Patriarch, Athenagoras, is always careful to toe the official Turkish line and present himself to the world as a loyal Turkish citizen. When touring Greece in the summer of 1963 he spoke publicly of Turkey as "my country", which somewhat naturally infuriated his Greek audiences. When the two Phanariot bishops visited Rome in February 1965 to announce the decisions of the third Pan-Orthodox Conference to the Pope they did not fail to pay a courtesy call on the Turkish embassy in Rome.

One of the difficulties about the Patriarch's position in Istanbul is that despite the official line of the secular State that he is a simple citizen who also happens to be a local religious leader, he is still looked on by many Greeks in Istanbul as the Ethnarch, the final remaining pillar of Byzantium, the last stake in Greece's claim to

---

in the 1920s and has since been excommunicated by the Patriarchate.

[3] When he was elected, the present Patriarch, Athenagoras, was an American citizen. This was got round by saying that since his village of origin is in fact in Epirus, which prior to 1913 was in the Ottoman Empire, he was originally a Turkish subject. Today he has a Turkish passport.

"the City". The Turks, on a non-official level, see him as the symbol of detested Greekness in their midst, a colleague of Makarios who is making life impossible for their countrymen in Cyprus, at least as they see it.

Much of local Greek criticism of the present Patriarch arises from dissatisfaction with his conciliatory and diplomatic attitude towards official Turkey. It makes the local Greeks, and especially one of their newspapers, *Chronos*, see red when the Patriarchate is represented at Turkish celebrations for the anniversary of the fall of the city to the Ottoman Turks. They feel that Athenagoras is playing a double game when he sends a representative to Turkish celebrations for the death blow to the Byzantine Empire and then wears the robes and crown of a former Byzantine Emperor when singing Mass on Mount Athos (during the millenary celebrations on the Holy Mountain, 1963). He *is* playing a double game but is forced to do so by circumstances, however much this may hurt the *egoïsmós*[4] of the Greeks of Istanbul.

A further reason for the Patriarch's unpopularity in some quarters of the Greek community is his attempt to introduce liturgical reforms. When he first arrived from the United States in 1948 Athenagoras tried to introduce benches and organs into the churches in Istanbul and to do away with the shutting off of the altar from the view of the people at the most solemn moments of the Mass. These reforms met with fanatical opposition from many of the faithful who felt that once you start changing details, before you know where you are you have emptied the baby out with the bathwater and betrayed Orthodox tradition in important matters. Many of the Greeks of Istanbul have retained their distrust of Patriarch Athenagoras who tried (largely unsuccessfully) to introduce unholy, Catholic things like organs into Orthodox churches.

The Patriarch's second sphere of responsibility is his jurisdiction

---

[4] See p. 34 for explanation of "*egoïsmós*".

over Athos, the Greeks of Crete and Rhodes and those in Western Europe, America and Australia.[5] The Greek State left Athos, Crete and Rhodes in the Patriarchate's jurisdiction after their liberation from the Turks and the Italians (Rhodes from the Italians) instead of incorporating them into the Church of Greece, in order to bolster the prestige of Constantinople which had been progressively stripped of nearly all its dependencies. The most important area under the Patriarchate's jurisdiction is the Archbishopric of North and South America, grouping about one and a half million faithful. Though these communities of Greeks come directly under the Patriarchate they are not represented on the Patriarchal Synod. This is composed of twelve titular bishops permanently resident in Istanbul and elected to the Synod for life; they have to be Turkish citizens. This arrangement is remarkably undemocratic for an Orthodox Church and is due as much to the closed, coterie set-up in the Phanar as to Turkish regulations. All the bishops, arch-secretaries, secretaries, etc., in the Patriarch's entourage are old boys of the theological institute of Halki. A Halki theological course is the only entry into the Phanar. It is unfortunate that Greek Orthodox all over the world should be ruled by a Synod of bishops who have no direct contact with their particular diaspora problems and equally unfortunate for the Phanar group that they should be deprived of the breath of fresh air the bishops from Europe, Australia and America could supply. The picture is not quite as black as I have painted it since the bishops from these places pay frequent visits to Istanbul and keep the Patriarch briefed on what is going on in their provinces; furthermore, Athenagoras himself spent fifteen years as Archbishop of North and South America and has a clear idea of the problems besetting the Orthodox in the West.

[5] Theoretically Northern Greece is still under the spiritual jurisdiction of the Patriarchate, but, with the exception of Athos, this area may be regarded as a fully integrated part of the Church of Greece.

It is impossible to get an officially confirmed idea of how the Patriarchate is financed. A visit to the Phanar itself would suggest that moneywise the place is hanging on by a thread. It stands a fifteen-minutes taxi ride from the centre of Istanbul in a slummy area a hundred yards or so back from the grimy quays and warehouses of the Golden Horn. In late 1963 the buildings, with the notable exception of the church, were unpainted and uncared for. The interior was equally unprepossessing : the carpets on the stairs were worn and threadbare, the edges of the doors round the handles were smudged with dirty finger marks and the only room I saw in a reasonable state of upkeep was the Patriarch's own study. The sad appearance of the Patriarchal residence is due both to policy and carelessness. All the minorities in Istanbul (Greek, Armenian and Jewish) try to avoid signs of material ostentation so as not to feed the fires of Turkish xenophobia. On the other hand, there would be nothing ostentatious about keeping the place decently clean. (In contrast to the Phanar the theological school is housed in a spacious, well-kept modern building on the top of a hill on the island of Halki, off Istanbul.) If the Phanarial buildings suggest lack of funds the bishops' ample salaries and their frequent holiday trips abroad do not. As far as can be ascertained, the Patriarchate's income includes the offerings of the Greeks of the city, a discreet subsidy from the Greek Government, a percentage of candle money, etc., taken by the Church in Crete and Rhodes, and an annual collection in the United States. Financially, then, the area under the Patriarchate's jurisdiction outside Istanbul is of considerable importance.

The Patriarch's third sphere of responsibility is as Ecumenical Patriarch, the head, *honoris causa*, of world Orthodoxy. The Second and Fourth Ecumenical Councils recognized Constantinople and Rome as having "equal privileges". After the 1054 schism Constantinople became the first ranking patriarchate in the Eastern half of Christendom, backed by the political power of

Byzantium. When the city fell to the Turks the effective power of Constantinople outside the confines of the Ottoman domains was reduced, but in the long run the Patriarch's first ranking continued to be recognized, in spite of rebellious rumblings from Moscow. Today the Patriarch's first ranking amounts to the following four rights: (i) when concelebrating Mass with other Patriarchs Constantinople has the right to the first place; (ii) Constantinople has the right of arbitration in case of dispute between two other Orthodox Churches (this right was last used in the nineteenth century)—the Patriarch's role is an interpretive one—he can act as a referee when invited to do so but cannot interfere or legislate with regard to matters outside his own province; (iii) Constantinople has the exclusive right of convening Pan-Orthodox Conferences—Athenagoras revived this right by calling the first Rhodes Conference to deal with matters internal to Orthodoxy and the second and third Rhodes Conferences to decide on Orthodoxy's relations with the non-Orthodox Christian Churches; (iv) Constantinople has the right to represent Orthodoxy in dealings with the "heterodox".

It is difficult for a Westerner not to think of the Ecumenical Patriarch as a sort of Eastern equivalent to the Pope. The parallel often subconsciously drawn between the Roman primacy and the Ecumenical Patriarch's first ranking vitiates any chance of understanding the Patriarch's position in world Orthodoxy. The Pope has administrative and doctrinal jurisdiction over the whole of the Catholic Church—since Vatican I he can pronounce on dogmatic matters and his pronouncements are binding on the whole Catholic Church. In Orthodoxy the supreme administrative authority is not vested in the Ecumenical Patriarch, but in the hierarchies of the separate autocephalous Churches. Supreme authority in matters of doctrine and canon law does not belong to the Ecumenical Patriarch, but to the Ecumenical Councils at which all the autocephalous Churches are represented. The last of these was held in the ninth century. The power of the Pope may be roughly compared to that of the President of the United States of America, while the role of the Ecumenical Patriarch is similar to that of a Secretary-General of the U.N. (if pushed too far the comparison becomes fallacious).

Another difference between the positions of the Pope and the Ecumenical Patriarch is in the composition of their respective entourages. However great the preponderance of its Italian element the Vatican is still a ruling body of international character while the Phanar is an exclusively Greek institution. The Vatican has to be, at least to some extent, international since it has direct jurisdiction over Catholics of all nations and races. The Phanar has no jurisdiction of any sort over the Slav Orthodox, the Rumanian Orthodox, the Arab Orthodox or the African Orthodox. As its jurisdiction is almost exclusively over Greeks it is not surprising that its composition should be Greek.

The main challenge to Constantinople's first ranking has traditionally come from Russia. Until 1448 the head of the Russian Church was appointed by Constantinople and was often a Greek. In that year a council of the local bishops elected a Russian as head of the Russian Church without consulting Constantinople. The Russian Church thus became autocephalous. At about the same time, in the middle of the fifteenth century, the Russians finally threw off the Tartar yoke, while Byzantium succumbed to the Turks.

With the independence of the Russian Church, the rise of Moscow as capital and the fall of Constantinople, was born the idea of Moscow as the "Third Rome". The Grand Duke of Moscow began to assume the Byzantine titles of "Autocrat" and "Tsar" (a corruption of Caesar) and to use the double-headed eagle of Constantinople as his State emblem. The Russian train of thought was that the first Rome had been overrun by the barbarians and then fallen into heresy; Constantinople, the second

Rome, had fallen into heresy at the unionistic Council of Florence and in punishment God had delivered her over to the Turks. From then on Moscow was to be the third Rome, the centre of Eastern Christendom.

Today the Patriarchate of Moscow officially recognizes Constantinople's first ranking in the Orthodox world, but a tense rivalry still exists between the two sees. While recognizing Constantinople's first ranking the Russian Church is clearly determined that first ranking should not be taken to mean leadership of world Orthodoxy. This has been especially evident in Russian reaction to Constantinople's initiatives *vis-à-vis* Rome. On 6 December 1963 Patriarch Athenagoras announced publicly that he would like a meeting of the heads of the Christian Churches to take place in the Holy Land at the time of the Pope's pilgrimage there. Rome reacted favourably, but before he could go to Jerusalem Athenagoras felt he had to get the telegraphic approval of the heads of the autocephalous Churches. Patriarch Alexis of Moscow's reply was that he regarded the meeting of the Pope and the Ecumenical Patriarch "not as a Church summit meeting but as a meeting between two important churchmen" and added that had ill health not precluded it he would have liked to attend the meeting himself. In other words, in the eyes of the Russian Church Athenagoras met the Pope as "an important churchman" but not as the leader of world Orthodoxy.

In the course of the third Pan-Orthodox Conference at Rhodes in November 1964 the Russian Church made clear that while she allows Constantinople first ranking in matters of protocol she in no way accepts the latter as the effective leader of Orthodoxy. In his first speech to the Conference the head of the Russian delegation, Archbishop Nikodim, was careful to point out that while it was the Ecumenical Patriarch who had convoked the Conference this had happened as a result of a letter sent to him by Patriarch Alexis of Moscow suggesting such a step. Nikodim wanted it to be clear that the prime initiative for convoking the Conference was Moscow's, not Constantinople's.

An important paragraph in the Third Rhodes Conference's decisions states that though time is needed to prepare suitable conditions before an Orthodox–Catholic dialogue can be opened "this does not mean that any of the local Orthodox Churches is precluded from continuing the cultivation of sisterly relations with the Roman Catholic Church, providing she does this on her own behalf and not in the name of all Orthodoxy. . . ." This paragraph gives Constantinople freedom of ecumenical action but at the same time cuts her down to size. Russia wanted it to be clear that in her overtures to Rome Constantinople was not acting as a sort of Eastern Rome but as one of fifteen or so local autocephalous Churches.

It was only after a great struggle and committees sitting all night that the Constantinople delegation won their point that the Conference's decision in favour of a dialogue at an undefined time after the end of Vatican II should be communicated to the Pope by the Ecumenical Patriarch. Up till the last minute the Russians insisted that all that needed to happen was for a copy of the Conference's decisions to be sent by the Conference's chairman to Cardinal Bea, head of the Vatican secretariat for Christian Unity. Only at the last minute did the Russians give in on this point, thus allowing Constantinople a face-saving concession and an affirmation of her right to represent Orthodoxy in dealings with the "heterodox".

What future lies in store for the Ecumenical Patriarchate? The main factor in trying to answer this question is whether or not the Patriarchate will continue in Istanbul. At first sight there seems every reason for moving the Phanar to somewhere it could function efficiently in a non-hostile atmosphere. In Istanbul it has been buffeted by the back-wash of each successive Cyprus crisis which, besides producing a siege mentality in the Phanariots, much reduces their scope for efficient action. The Turkish authorities are waging a war of slow attrition against what most Turks regard as this last bastion of hated imperial Byzantium. Recent examples of harrying action on the part of the Turkish authorities have been : (i) their near refusal to grant the Patriarch a passport for his journey to the Athos millenary celebration (June 1963); (ii) the expulsion of two senior Phanariot bishops from Turkey (April 1964); (iii) the closing down (spring 1964) of the Patriarchal printing presses and thus the silencing of *Apostolos Andreas*, the Patriarchate's official journal; (iv) threats to demolish the outer wall of the Phanar on "town planning grounds", etc. There can be little doubt that Turkey would like to see the Patriarchate die little by little of sheer inanition. As already mentioned, exclusive entry to the Phanar's hierarchy is through the college of Halki. The Turkish authorities have stipulated that not more than 35 per cent of each year's intake to the college may come from outside Turkey. As less and less Orthodox with Turkish nationality enter the college, since the Greek population of Istanbul has declined steadily over the last twenty years, the 35 per cent rule threatens to strangle the college by cutting off the supply of Greeks from Greece. Who will there then be to staff the Phanar as the older bishops die off? All the evidence seems to point to the advisability of the Patriarchate being speedily moved to a more neutral or favourable environment.

There are, however, at least two weighty arguments against such a move. The first is that it would be impossible for the Patriarch to desert his flock in Istanbul at a time of danger and difficulty. His mere presence among them suffices to arouse world opinion against maltreatment of them by the Turks. The desertion of the flock argument gets less valid as the Orthodox population shrinks with more and more people migrating to Greece; in 1945 there were 110,000 Greeks in Turkey and now there are just over 60,000. However, as long as there are Greeks in Istanbul, no matter how few, it is certain that any plan to move the Patriarchate elsewhere would be greeted by accusations of betrayal from all over the Greek-speaking world.

The second argument against moving the Patriarchate is that it is unthinkable for the Patriarch to reside anywhere else than in the old imperial city and that his prestige, on which his position in Orthodoxy so much depends, would evaporate if he took up residence in Rhodes, Athos or New York (three places sometimes mentioned in discussion of where the Phanar could be moved to). This argument is imbued with historical emotionalism but is nonetheless powerful for that. If one imagines the reactions of the Catholics to a proposal to move the Vatican from Rome had Italy gone communist after the war, one gains some insight into how the Orthodox, especially the Greeks, feel about the idea of moving the Patriarchate from Constantinople where it has been for seventeen centuries. This feeling is nowhere stronger than in the Phanar itself, even though the younger, more open-minded bishops and theologians realize that the situation is getting more and more untenable. A great fear among those who, on practical grounds, might wish to see the Patriarchate moved is that perhaps Russia would claim that Moscow was the Ecumenical Patriarchate once the Church of Constantinople was geographically no longer the Church of Constantinople. Despite all the practical desirability of moving the Ecumenical Patriarchate out of a hostile backwater where its work on the international level is constantly hampered and where its very existence is imperilled, the risks of a move at the present time seem too great to those who would have to make it. Barring unexpected developments, the Phanar is likely to remain for some time yet in its Istanbul slum.

CONSTANTINOPLE, GENEVA AND ROME

The Patriarchate was in right at the start of the Ecumenical Movement that finally led to the founding of the World Council f Churches (W.C.C.). As early as 1920, in the encyclical "Unto he Churches of Christ wheresoever they be", the Patriarchate uggested the setting up of a League of Churches on the lines of he League of Nations. The member Churches would gradually ome to know and love each other in the following ways: by ccepting a uniform calendar so that the celebration of the great Christian feasts be on the same day in all Christian Churches (the najority of the Orthodox still follow today the old Julian calendar), y an exchange of brotherly letters on great feasts, by contact between theologians and exchange of books, periodicals and students, by impartial examination of doctrinal differences, by the Churches allowing each other the use of places of prayer and cemetery facilities where necessary, by the settlement of the mixed marriage question, and finally by collaboration of all the member Churches in the work of strengthening religious belief, organizing charitable projects, etc. The Patriarchate was represented at all the inter-war and post-World War II conferences that led up to the founding of the World Council of Churches in 1948. Today Constantinople is a full member of the W.C.C. while, like other Orthodox Churches which are members, reserving the right not to sign the communiqués issued by the W.C.C.'s Faith and Order Conferences, which discuss doctrinal matters.

Since he became Patriarch in 1948, Athenagoras has done all he can to increase the Patriarchate's participation in the work of the W.C.C. He felt that the first thing was for the Orthodox to learn what the W.C.C. was, so in 1951 he instituted a course at the college of Halki on the history of the Ecumenical Movement. In an encyclical in 1952 he suggested that all the Orthodox Churches should set up a regular committee to co-ordinate their participation in the W.C.C. This did not prove possible, but the Orthodox delegations to the Faith and Order committee of the W.C.C. are able to maintain a united front on doctrinal matters since in this field there are no cleavages between them.

In his support for the W.C.C. Patriarch Athenagoras is carrying on the tradition of his predecessors—the two great innovational achievements of his reign so far have been the re-establishment of contact between the autocephalous Orthodox Churches and his immediate and courageous reaction to recent changes in the attitude of Rome to the other Christian Churches. As suggested in Chapter 7 a necessary presupposition to dialogue between the Catholics and the Orthodox is that the latter should present themselves as one united Church and not as fifteen or so national Churches, each pursuing its own separate policy in ecumenical matters. Thus both Athenagoras's outstanding achievements, restoring contact among the Orthodox and making contact with the Catholic Church, must be regarded as substantial steps towards the *rapprochement* of Orthodoxy and Catholicism.

The Patriarch's achievements are all the more remarkable when one considers the set-up in which he lives. The men in the Phanar consist of a majority who do very little, largely owing to lack of organization, and a minority who are worked off their feet. Those who carry the burden of the Patriarchate's business are at times of stress reduced to a state of near exhaustion. One of the results of this state of affairs is that the Patriarch has centralized everything into his own hands. It is said that he even sees to details as minor as paying the taxi bills of guests leaving the Phanar. As a result he too is often grossly overworked. He is a man of very strong personality and dominates the other bishops—this has enabled him to proceed in ecumenical matters probably faster than some of the older members of the Synod would have liked. For instance, in June 1964 the Patriarch received Maximos IV, Patriarch of the Melkite Uniats, despite strong anti-Uniat feeling in the Phanar Athenagoras receives active support on ecumenical affairs from some of the younger bishops and from the lay theologians of the Halki College. Halki is the ecumenical power house of the Patriarchate and lay theologians are always included in the Patriarcha delegations to conferences abroad. Two of the lay theologians in particular are known to be the Patriarch's close advisers on ecumenical matters.

Athenagoras's achievements are due to a combination of an impulsive, outgoing heart and an almost fox-like diplomatic astuteness. An excellent example of this combination was the preparation for his meeting with the Pope. He reacted spontaneously and warmly to the announcement of the Pope's pilgrimage—it genuinely moved him to hear that the Roman Pontiff was going as a humble pilgrim to pray on the Mount of Olives. At the same time he saw that he would have to get the approval of the other Orthodox Churches before any meeting between himself and the Pope could take place. Then, as already noted, instead of consulting them first and subsequently announcing his desire to meet the Pope, he made the public announcement immediately and only then wired the various Orthodox Churches. This timing made it much more difficult for them to say no since such a refusal would have projected an image of Orthodox disunity across the World. In this way the Patriarch was able to meet the Pope with the semi-approval of world Orthodoxy. Had he acted less astutely the other Orthodox Churches might well have succeeded in curbing his generous enthusiasm.

To what extent has Patriarch Athenagoras managed to renew contact among the autocephalous Orthodox Churches? The renewal of contact has come about in two ways: by the heads of the various Churches paying one another visits and by the convening of Pan-Orthodox Conferences. Patriarch Athenagoras himself has toured the Near Eastern Patriarchates and Greece, while most of the heads of the Slav Churches, including Patriarch Alexis of Russia, have visited him in the Phanar. The Athos millenary celebrations in 1963 provided a further opportunity for a meeting between the heads of the Churches. The exchange of visits between patriarchs has opened the way for inter-Orthodox contact on a

F

lower, broader level. Early in 1964 a group of Russian priests and theologians on their way to the Holy Land spent a week in Athens and in the autumn of the same year a group of Salonica theologians visited Russia. The growing consciousness among younger Greek theologians of the existence and importance of the non-Greek Orthodox Churches (see Chapter 7) is another result of the climate produced by the renewal of contact between the Churches at leader level.

The First Pan-Orthodox Conference in 1961 was a great triumph for the Ecumenical Patriarch. For the first time in centuries the Orthodox Churches were gathered in one place to discuss the setting of their house in order. The Conference's main result was agreement on an agenda for a future pro-synod, a sort of Orthodox *aggiornamento* council. In a way the triumph of the First Rhodes Conference lay not so much in its results as in the fact that it had proved possible to hold it at all, with Slavs, Rumanians, Arabs (Antioch) and Greeks all sitting round the same table. The Second Conference (1963) dealt with Orthodox–Catholic relations and the Third with Orthodoxy's relations with the Catholics, Old Catholics and Anglicans. In the last two Conferences the final decisions were reached unanimously, and this is genuinely an achievement for the Orthodox Church torn as it is by national rivalries and cut in two by the Iron Curtain. The Conferences have discovered the formula of leaving matters that cannot be unanimously agreed on to the conscience of each individual Church. The Second Conference could not agree on whether observers should be sent to the Vatican Council and so decided that this was a matter for each Church to decide for herself. The Third Conference could not agree on the content and timing of a dialogue with Rome and so decided, as we have already mentioned, that for the time being each Church may "continue the cultivation of sisterly relations with the Roman Catholic Church, providing she does this on her own behalf and not in the name of all Orthodoxy . . .". Quite

part from the intrinsic importance of the decisions reached
y the Conferences they have done immense good by allowing
Greek and Slav church intellectuals to meet each other, get to
now something of each other's problems and size each other
p. This internal stock-taking by the Orthodox is absolutely neces-
ary if there is to be a viable Orthodox–Catholic dialogue in the
uture.

What of Constantinople's own ecumenism? As early as 1954 the
'atriarch was talking of his hopes for "unity" (*enótis*) between the
Orthodox and Catholic Churches. Athenagoras has grafted a
pecial meaning on to the word "unity"—he sees it not as unity in
aith and organization but unity in spirit and purpose, in other
vords friendly co-operation with the Catholic Church of the sort
nat already exists between the Orthodox and the Protestants in
ne W.C.C. He has always spoken of "union" (*enósis*) as being a
istant goal. However, this has not stopped Constantinople pressing
or the opening of a theological dialogue with Rome. At the Third
hodes Conference the delegation from the City led the camp
nat wanted to define the content and the timing of the dialogue.
The other camp, led by the Russians, wanted to postpone the dis-
ussion of the content and timing until after the end of the Vatican
Council—it was their view that finally won the day.) In his first
peech to the Conference the Phanariot Bishop Chrysostomos of
Myra told the delegates that: (i) the whole world knows of the
econd Conference's decision that in principle there should be a
Catholic–Orthodox dialogue and expects an initiative on our part;
i) the announcement of the dialogue is the next step after the
ope–Patriarch meeting and the sending of observers to the
Vatican Council (by Moscow and Constantinople); (iii) failure to
nnounce the dialogue would be regarded as fear of discussion
ith the Western Church; (iv) if no announcement is made the
econd Conference's decision to initiate a dialogue will look like
decision to initiate a monologue.

Though the Conference's decisions[6] were much less positiv than Constantinople would have liked, this in no way dampene the ecumenical enthusiasm of the Patriarchal delegation. Speakin in Patras after the end of the Conference on 18 November 196. Bishop Meliton, head of the Constantinople delegation, said : "A regards the Catholic Church the Conference has decided that w should immediately start a dialogue of love to further the cultiv. tion of sisterly feelings between the local Orthodox Churches an the Catholic Church. At Rhodes we decided to prepare our flocl to start seeing their Roman Catholic brothers as brothers and *no* as strangers." To grasp how deeply imbued with the ecumenic. spirit the above speech is, one only has to compare it with the ant ecumenical Archbishop of Athens' reaction to the Conference. H found its decisions to be "entirely satisfactory", interpreting the as a pause in ecumenical activity : "We await an indication good will on the part of the Vatican, which, as yet, we have n received. The head of the Roman Catholic Church continues insist on his prerogatives, 'primacy' and 'infallibility'. . . . such conditions a dialogue on equal terms is not easy. The Co. ference was right to decide that before any dialogue is begun the

[6] The text of the Third Pan-Orthodox Conference's decisions stated th Orthodoxy desires good relations with all the other Christian Churches so to bring about the unity of Christians everywhere in the one, holy, cathol and apostolic Church. In this spirit the First Rhodes Conference decided the cultivation of relations with other Christian Churches and the Secor Rhodes Conference decided in principle that there should be a dialogue equal terms with the Roman Catholic Church. The text went on : "T Third-Pan Orthodox Conference repeats the Orthodox Church's previous expressed wish with regard to a dialogue. After study of the factors involve the Conference has come to the conclusion that proper preparation and t creation of suitable conditions are necessary for the opening of a genui theological dialogue. This, however, does not mean that any of the loc Orthodox Churches is precluded from continuing the cultivation of sister relations with the Roman Catholic Church, providing she does this on h own behalf and not in the name of all Orthodoxy, in the conviction that this way the difficulties at present existing may be neutralized. . . ."

must be due preparation and the creation of suitable conditions."

Patriarch Athenagoras has made Constantinople the spearhead of ecumenism from the Orthodox side. It is unlikely that his successor would want to or be able to alter this situation. For all that, however, the Patriarch is well aware that he cannot go more than one or two steps faster than the Iron Curtain Churches and the Church of Greece.

It was made clear at the Third Rhodes Conference that it is much more difficult for the Churches behind the Iron Curtain to be ecumenically minded than for the Greeks who live in the comparatively freer world. Ecclesiastically the Slavs and Rumanians are isolated and are consequently much less well informed as to developments in the non-Orthodox world. The main task of these hierarchies is to see that Orthodoxy survives its daily persecution by the State. For example, it would clearly have been foolish for the Russian delegation at the Third Rhodes Conference to have seemed too well disposed towards *rapprochement* with Rome before the Vatican Council's final views on atheism had been pronounced.

Apart from political considerations, which to the Slavs and Rumanians mean the survival or not of their Churches, many delegates at the Conference expressed their disappointment with the results achieved by the first two and a half sessions of the Vatican Council in the strictly religious field. The Bulgarian delegates told me they were very disappointed with the Council text on the collegiality of the bishops : they felt it to be studded with references to the power of the Pope. The Rumanian Bishop Justin of Moldavia told the delegates that the 1963 Conference had decided on a dialogue because it had then been thought that the Catholic Church would revise certain of her views, but it does not seem that this is in fact happening. The Rumanian bishop demanded that the two Churches be recognized as equals and that an end be put to the action of the Uniats and to proselytism. The head

of the Polish delegation, Bishop Stefan of Bielostok, complained
that his faithful had suffered persecution by the Polish Catholic
Church as much as by the State. Consequently he recommended
caution in all dealings with Rome. The Yugoslav Bishop
Damascene of Zagreb stressed that the faithful in his country had
not been prepared for the idea of *rapprochement* with the Catholics. (This is a discreet understatement since during the last war
the Croatian Catholics murdered 750,000 Serbian Orthodox and
executed 500 Orthodox priests.) For various reasons, then, varying
from country to country, it is not easy for the Orthodox behind the
Iron Curtain to be as ecumenically minded as their Greek co-
religionists.

As we have seen earlier in the book, though there are many
indications that the Greeks of Greece are gradually becoming more
open to the ecumenical spirit, it is the Synod and the hierarchy that
take the decisions and in recent years the most conservative faction
among the Greek bishops has usually been dominant. Patriarch
Athenagoras of Constantinople needs all his skill if he is to edge
forward in the *rapprochement* with Rome without breaking the
fragile web of Orthodox unity woven in the first five years of the
'sixties.

9

catholic ecumenism and the greeks

IN THE preceding chapters an attempt has been made to give a detailed picture of ecumenical attitudes in the various sectors of the Church of Greece. Accepting the risk that generalization tends to over-simplify complicated patterns of thought and emotion, this final chapter will attempt to look at Catholic ecumenism as it appears to educated, religiously interested, Orthodox people in Greece.

The more overtly intended ecumenical actions of the Catholic Church like the Pope's readiness to meet the Patriarch, the return of various relics to the East (the Apostle Andrew, St Sabbas, St Titus), and the magnificent gesture of Cardinal Bea kneeling humbly in prayer in Sancta Sophia, Istanbul, where Cardinal Humbert had arrogantly laid the act of excommunication against the Patriarch on the altar in 1054, have made a deep impression on the Greeks.[1] The Eastern experts in the Vatican Secretariat for Christian Unity are well aware of the importance of symbol to the Greek mind and these symbolic acts of reparation for wrongs done to the East by the West in the past attack the Greek historical feeling of injury *vis-à-vis* Rome at its roots.

Naturally enough, however, the Greeks do not judge Catholic ecumenism only on those gestures inspired by the Unity secretariat which are most overtly aimed at conciliating the East. To the

---

[1] Cardinal Bea's gesture was clearly a major step towards the solemn revocation of the excommunications served by Rome on Constantinople and *vice versa* in 1054. On 7 December 1965 Pope Paul in Rome and the Ecumenical Patriarch in Constantinople solemnly annulled the anathemas their predecessors had hurled at each other 900 years previously.

Greeks the views and final decisions of the Vatican Council, taken
as a whole, are just as important, if not more so, when judging how
real the new Catholic ecumenism is and how deep it goes inside
the Catholic Church. While admitting that the Vatican Council is
something internal to the Catholic world, they rightly consider that
the mood it sets is of great relevance to ecumenism.

Is the new Catholic ecumenism launched in *Ecclesiam suam*
and *De oecumenismo* humble and sincere? This is a question that
troubles many thinking Orthodox people. They feel that Protestant ecumenism originated in a realization of lack, inadequacy,
and in a genuine search for spiritual fulfilment. Catholic ecumenism, though a step forward from the previous "*non possumus*"
attitude, still seems to be based on the concept that Catholicism is
the ideal form of Christianity in every respect, though now non-
Catholic Christians are politely referred to as "separated brethren"
instead of schismatics or heretics and contact with them is encouraged. The implication of the phrase "separated brethren" as
applied to Eastern Christians, that it was the Orthodox who broke
away from the Catholics, is impossible for the Orthodox to accept.
They feel that it is their Church which has retained the basic
teachings, practices and mentality of the early Church. Whether
one characterizes the path taken by Western Christianity from the
time of Charlemagne on as marked by harmful innovations or
natural developments depends on whether one is an Orthodox or
a Catholic, but historically and objectively speaking there is no
doubt that the changes have occurred in the West and not in the
East. It is the West that has moved (the *filioque*, the growth of the
Papacy, the Thomist take-over bid of theology) and the East that
has remained stationary. To maintain that the East split off from
the West is to imply movement where there was none. Therefore
the Orthodox have certain objective, historical grounds for object-
ing to being called "separated brethren".

They also object to the term on the grounds that if they are "separated" this implies that the aim of Catholic ecumenism is that they should "return". Indeed the Pope said as much in his Bethlehem speech on 6 January 1964, the day after he met the Ecumenical Patriarch; preaching at Bethlehem the Pope urged the "separated brethren" to return to "the fold of the Catholic Church". The editorial heading in the Athenian newspaper *Ethnos* on 7 January, "Union not submission", was typical of Greek reaction to the speech. To the Orthodox way of thinking reunion conceived of as a "return" to Catholicism can mean nothing else than the submission of Orthodoxy to Rome, the swallowing up of the semi-democratic ecclesiology of the East by the autocratic system of the West. The more conservative Orthodox maintain that on the contrary Catholicism must return to Orthodoxy; sometimes this view is expressed by saying that both Churches must return to the teachings and practices of the Early Church—it comes to much the same thing. A few really ecumenically-minded Orthodox like Agouridis and Alivizatos feel that both Churches have made serious mistakes in the past—they must admit them, repent of them and get together in rectifying them.

To the Greek Orthodox the idea of "submission" to Rome is not a vague, intellectual speculation about the future, but a sharp, emotionally coloured memory from the past. In the thirteenth century when the crusaders ruled Greece they summarily suppressed the Greek hierarchy and replaced them with Latin bishops. Cyprus spent three centuries in "submission" to Rome and as a result almost welcomed the invading Turk who restored an Eastern hierarchy. The history books remind each generation of young Orthodox of these unpleasant facts and it is not surprising that the "separated brethren" formula should make many Orthodox uneasy if they see in it hints of *ipotagí* (submission).

It was clearly in order to rule out the suspicion that dialogue with Rome might be a prologue to "submission" that the Second Pan-Orthodox Conference decided that eventual dialogue must take place on "an equal footing". Professor Alivizatos defines this as meaning that one section of the Church has the democratic right to examine and criticize the other sections of the Church without this right giving rise to pretensions of superiority—the examination should be conducted as a brotherly duty. There is clearly a wide gap between the concept of mutual criticism on a democratic and brotherly basis and the notions of "separated brethren" and "return to the fold".

Besides the doubts about the humility of the new Catholic ecumenism outlined above there are even more serious doubts about its sincerity. The Orthodox rather naturally are surprised by attitudes on the part of Rome that seem to be self-contradictory. If Rome really wants to open a dialogue with the East why does she lay such stress on the greatest bone of contention between the two Churches, the primacy? In 1964 the Pope's Bethlehem speech, *Ecclesiam suam* and the pontifical opening speech at the third session of the Council all laid heavy stress on the primacy. Those Orthodox who have a picture of the Catholic Church as a whole realize that the Pope was at that time under severe pressure from conservative Catholic quarters. The majority, however, see the repeated assertion of the primacy and the simultaneous extension of a hand of friendship to the East as so difficult to comprehend as to be suspicious.

Was the Vatican Council sincere when at the end of the third session it promulgated *De oecumenismo* (in tone, at least, pleasing to Orthodox ears), and the Eastern Churches decree confirming and strengthening Uniatism (considered by the Orthodox to be a thorn in their flesh)?

We dealt with the question of the Uniats in Greece in a footnote in Chapter 5, but something more must be said about them in the context of Catholic ecumenism. The Greek Uniats, who admit that until World War II they were engaged in proselytizing the Orthodox, today maintain that they are a bridge between Western

Catholicism and the Orthodox East. They say they present the Greeks with a picture of Catholicism in action on three levels, theological, liturgical and practical. On the theological level they maintain that it is easier for a priest conversant with Eastern theology to present Catholic thinking to the Orthodox. (The Uniats do a course in Eastern theology over and above the normal Western seminary theology course.) On the liturgical level the Uniats maintain that they present Catholicism in its genuine Eastern form, in the language of the New Testament and not disguised under the unnatural garb of Latin. Dressed exactly like Orthodox Pappádes they celebrate Mass in a way that renders it indistinguishable from the Orthodox Mass. On the practical level the Uniats have shown themselves to be tireless social workers, having founded a hospital, student hostels and orphanages.

To the overwhelming majority of the Orthodox, however, the removal of the Uniat bishop and twenty or so priests from Greece would be the most cast-iron proof Rome could give of her ecumenical sincerity. The Orthodox find it extremely difficult to believe that proselytism has really stopped. Even those who admit the compelling evidence that points to this being the case still feel the Uniats must go. They feel that if the Uniats are full Catholics, recognizing the primacy and infallibility of the Pope as at present defined, they should not dress up as Orthodox, wear beards and cylindrical hats and mislead people by saying a Mass identical with the Orthodox one. If they are really Eastern Christians they should join the Orthodox Church. Bishop after bishop and theologians all over Greece have told me, usually unprompted, of what they feel to be the "scandal of Uniatism". Ecumenically speaking, however uncomprehending and prejudiced the Orthodox dislike for the Uniats may be, its universality and in some cases its passion make the Greek Uniats' claim to be a bridge between Catholicism and Orthodoxy in Greece complete nonsense. On the contrary, in the present atmosphere, their presence is one of the most serious obstacles to Orthodox–Catholic *rapprochement* in Greece. (This judgment is confined to Greece—the situation of the Uniats in the Near East is somewhat different.)

Naturally, then, the Greeks find it difficult to understand how the third session of the Vatican Council could in the same breath proclaim the ecumenical decree and the Eastern Churches decree. The perplexed Orthodox is once again left with the question: Is Catholic ecumenism sincere? In the light of the Eastern Churches decree which reinforces the position of the Uniats and appears to the Greeks as an unecumenical act on the practical level, what is to be made of apparently ecumenically inspired gestures like the return of relics to their former resting places in the East? The Orthodox with inside knowledge of the Catholic Church realize that these inconsistencies are the result of seething and sometimes contradictory change in the Western Church—in one case the conservative element carries the day while in another the progressives come out on top. To less well informed Greeks, the majority, these inconsistencies are reasons for doubting the uprightness of the new Catholic ecumenism.

If the ecumenical spirit in Greece is to gain ground Catholic ecumenism must show itself to be both humble and sincere. The Catholic Church must fully accept that an eventual dialogue should take place "on an equal footing", with all that phrase implies. Despite the historical memories working against a softening of the Orthodox attitude towards Rome and the latent fanaticism that is part of the Greek psychological make-up, the ground in Greece is ready for the further growth of ecumenical attitudes. The rising standard of education, urbanization, the increase of residence abroad (especially in Germany), the growing consciousness of Europe and its ways of thinking are all factors that are freeing the Greek from his over-absorption in the Byzantine past. Catholic ecumenism must work in such a way as to help rather than hinder the task of Orthodox ecumenists like Professor Alivizatos, determined to dissipate the feelings of hate the Greeks have inherited from their past. In the Professor's own words: "The centuries and their harsh happenings have left us with indifference, suspicion, enmity, hate, crimes and fanaticism. The dialogue of love must look this legacy in the face and completely wipe it away. . . ."

report on the orthodox church in bulgaria

ORTHODOXY is the majority religion in Bulgaria with about six million baptized Orthodox in a population of seven and a half million. The only other sizeable religious group are the Muslims with 600,000. As in Greece the resurgence of national conscious-ness after 400 years of Turkish rule began among the Church intellectuals in the late eighteenth and early nineteenth centuries. Bulgarian nationalism and the Orthodox Church are closely linked in the minds of the people and the Communists have avoided a head-on collision with the Church. The 1949 law on religions grants the Orthodox Church semi-official status—its third article states : "The Bulgarian Orthodox Church is the inherited religion of the Bulgarian people and therefore linked with its history, and as such the Church is allowed, in accordance with its essence and spirit, to be the Church of the Bulgarian People's Republic." This semi-official status is not merely theoretical—each month the Com-munist State pays the salaries of the country's 2,000 active Orthodox priests and the pensions of a large number of older ones. The Theological Academy is still allowed to occupy an imposing block in one corner of Lenin Square, Sophia's central square. Within ten minutes' walk from this square are more than half a dozen churches, some of them in prominent positions, which were all in use the Sunday I was there.

The Orthodox Church has had to accept a number of restrictions in order to achieve the apparently favourable status she possesses today. First and foremost she no longer has the right to provide religious instruction for the young (under eighteen). All religious teaching in primary and secondary schools has been suppressed and Sunday school for under eighteens is not permitted. As a result young people get only as much religious instruction as their parents can give them and as they can glean from the sermon and the Mass, if they go to church. Since the majority of the population is peasant (Sophia has a population approaching one million and Bulgaria's second town, Plovdiv, 200,000), few parents are in a position to teach their children much about religion. In the schools subjects such as history are taught with a Marxist–Leninist slant and the philosophy course at the end of secondary school consists in the main of Marxism—all candidates for the University have to sit an examination in the theory of Communism.

One of the results of the totally a-religious and in part anti-religious training provided in State schools is that very few of the students in the Theological Academy have come from such schools. Most of the Academy's 15–20 entrants each year come from the minor seminary of Tserepis, which at the moment has about 175 pupils doing the six-year course (about thirty per annum). The pupils from the seminary who do not go on to the Academy can become priests on completing their six-year course. The existence of one minor seminary and the Academy are a major concession which the State has made to the Orthodox but not to the Catholic Church in Bulgaria.[1] The concession is a vital one since the dribble of "half theologians" from the Tserepis seminary and of theologians from the Sophia Academy enables the Orthodox Church to ensure a supply of new priests. If the minor seminary

[1] There are 60,000 Latin rite Catholics in Bulgaria and 5,000 Uniats. When the Communists took over the country in 1944 they closed down the Catholic primary and secondary schools as well as the minor seminary at Plovdiv. The twenty or so Bulgarian seminarists studying in Italy during the 1941–44 period were not allowed to return and no young Bulgar has been allowed to study in Italy since. Unless this state of affairs alters the Catholic clergy in Bulgaria is doomed to extinction.

did not exist there would be almost no candidates for the Academy. The seminary's director, Bishop Tychon, told me that about a third of the boys come from "Levite" families, that is families in which the father or an uncle was a priest. However, in spite of the guaranteed trickle of entrants from Tserepis, the Sophia Academy now has only sixty to seventy students, compared with 200 before the war.

In the pre-1944 period Bulgarian theologians went West to specialize and mostly to Protestant theological faculties in Germany. Since 1944 the only place they have been able to go has been Moscow, with the exception of 1963 when two young theologians were allowed passports to go to Switzerland to study on World Council of Churches scholarships.

Through the various subsidies it grants the Church the State clearly has some control over what goes on in the Synod and its committees. The Church, however, is not completely dependent financially on the State. The monasteries and the eleven metropolitan sees have retained part of their former properties. I even visited a convent near the capital that had been founded since the Communist take-over. In 1950 there were five nuns and no buildings; by late 1964 there was a handsome three-storey building at Kniajevo, housing seventeen nuns (none of whom had come from other convents). There was difficulty in getting permission from the civil authorities to build, but after a struggle it was obtained. The money for the building came from the Holy Synod, the offerings of the local people and a gift from Patriarch Alexis of Moscow. In the whole country there are 120 monasteries and convents and about 500 monks and nuns. A monastery with five monks at Tserepis still owns 175 acres of grazing and farm land, and a convent I visited at Bistritza (near Sophia) owns twenty-two acres which are worked by its three nuns. They keep livestock. This is another concession by the State to the Church, since most of the land in rural Bulgaria has been collectivized.

Only a very few new churches have been built in Bulgaria since 1944, one of which I visited in a suburb of Sophia. The capital has a rapidly expanding population and many more churches are needed than it has been possible to build. However, repairs and redecoration of churches are a common sight in Bulgaria. In a village I went to, the interior of the church had been decorated with frescoes costing over £200, and in central Sophia I saw a large church façade undergoing extensive repairs. This suggests that article 7 of the 1949 law on religions is respected in practice. The article in question says that: "the religious communities (i.e. parishes) may build for their needs houses of prayer where they may freely conduct their religious services and liturgy". Trouble with the local Communist authorities over permission to build and repair churches does occur in distant parts of the country, but in the end, I was told, they too are brought to obey the law.

Do people in Bulgaria go to church? The answer is on the whole no, except on great feasts and for weddings, anniversaries, etc. In a village of 3,000 people near Sophia only seventy went to church on the first Sunday in December 1964. In this village there are only about 100 people who belong to the Communist party and they are sufficiently well disposed towards the local priest for the village council to have retimbered the upper half of the church's bell-tower. The priest told me that the Communist take-over had not affected the villagers' church-going habits. They did not go to church any more frequently before 1944 than they do today. On the other hand, he told me there had not been a single non-religious burial in the village in his thirty years as parish priest and most of the children are baptized. If one parent brings the child he christens it without asking questions—in this way the children of most of the Party members in the village are baptized Christians. There have been a number of cases in which villagers have contracted civil marriages only. This is normally because the man refuses to be married in church. In such cases the priest told me he does not deny the sacraments to the partner who wanted to be married in church but was unable to persuade the other.

I later asked the vicar-general of Sophia if the Orthodox Church in Bulgaria recognized civil marriage alone as valid. He told me that in certain cases she did, because it would be wrong to debar from the sacraments a woman whose husband had adamantly refused church marriage.

The Bulgarian Church is fortunate in that nearly all her 2,000-odd parish priests have at least been through the minor seminary, though this was not the case fifty years ago when a candidate taking his finals was asked:

"Who are the Protestants?"

"They are bad men."

"What is the Church?"

"The largest building in my village." He passed, but he wouldn't today. The relations between the local Communists and the Church depend very largely on the calibre of the parish priest. In one group of villages the authorities decided that the cemetery would be better away from the church on the edge of the village. The official reason given was hygiene, but the priest in one of the villages felt the real reason was the dissociation in people's minds of the cemetery from the church. He was highly respected in his community and in that village the cemetery stayed put—in all the surrounding villages the cemeteries have been moved.

The Bulgarian Orthodox Church publishes a religious weekly, *Tserkoven Vestnik* (circulation 4,000), and a heavy monthly, *Duhovna Kultura*, which sells 2,500 copies. Since the war a whole series of theological works have come off the Church presses, and in the religious bookshop five minutes' walk from Lenin Square I found copies of a vernacular version of the New Testament on sale at about 3s. 6d. A commission headed by a bishop is at present at work on a new edition of the complete Bible. The main weakness in the bookshop's display was the almost complete absence of popularly orientated booklets setting out the faith and explaining it in simple terms, the sort of book that in Greece is produced by *Zoi*. I was told that each diocesan town has a shop in which icons, books and religious objects generally are sold.

Although the State has allowed the Orthodox Church the semi-official status described above, this does not stop the Communist organizations engaging in virulent anti-religious propaganda. At least three renegade priests collaborating with the Communists have recently published anti-religious pamphlets. On the whole, however, lectures on atheism are as sparsely attended as church services. A Bulgar wishing to set his countrymen's ideological apathy in context told me : "The Russians are mystics, the Greeks are fanatics, but we are very down to earth." According to a well-informed Protestant source in Sophia at the time of my visit the majority of Bulgarians are indifferent equally to Christianity and atheism, a minority are religiously inclined and a tiny minority are actively anti-religious.

A certain number of parish priests—it was not possible to find out how many—are members of the Communist organized *Patriotic Front*. I asked various theologians if such priests were not compromising their vocations. The general feeling was that as long as they abstain from ideological gatherings their membership is a good thing for the Church. They do, however, speak alongside other local leaders, who are for the most part Communists, on national occasions such as the anniversary of the liberation of the country from the Turks. They also address meetings on the need for peace in the world. I remained sceptical but was told that if all the people in a village belong to the *Patriotic Front* and the priest persists in holding aloof his influence over them is much reduced, since he thus cuts himself out of a large part of the life of the community. One theologian quoted his own village of origin where the priest is an old man whose children have finished their education and left home and yet in 1963 he decided to join the

Front. He did not do it out of hope of personal gain for himself or for his family; he felt that membership would help his ministry. It is difficult to believe that all the priests who have joined the *Patriotic Front* have such blameless motives, but on the other hand it is all too easy for a Westerner to condemn as betrayal of the Church actions which may be a necessary part and parcel of co-existence with Communism.

In conclusion it may be said that the Bulgarian State treats the Orthodox Church with a strange mixture of restrictions and permissiveness. It forbids the religious education of the young, yet allows priests to be trained. It has atheism taught in the schools and yet it pays the salaries of the parish clergy. Graphic examples of this paradoxical treatment of the Orthodox Church are the disturbances that have occurred in recent years during the Easter vigil outside the Nevsky cathedral in Sophia. The normal pattern is that bands of young people, organized by the Communist youth movements, gather in the cathedral square and taunt those going to attend the service. Meanwhile inside the cathedral the priests, who are salaried employees of the Communist State, prepare to celebrate the Easter Mass.

ECUMENISM IN BULGARIA

There is considerable division of opinion in Bulgarian Orthodox circles as to the advisability and the usefulness of ecumenical contact with other Christian Churches. On the "extreme right" there are those who, like Bishop Parthenios of Levski, are fundamentally opposed to all contact with either Rome or the Protestants. In this group are two archimandrite monks, Sergei and Seraphim, who teach in the Theological Academy. The group has a small following, not more than 100 or so priests and monks, but its views are of consequence since its leaders are highly regarded theologians and since young men like Archimandrites Sergei and Seraphim are likely Synodical bishops of tomorrow.

The Patriarch Cyril and about ten of the eighteen Bulgarian bishops feel that some sort of contact with the other Churches is possible, but they are far from optimistic. The Patriarch has studied in Paris and is a specialist in Bulgarian Church history. He has recently published part one of a lengthy work on the activities of the Uniats in the Near East and Eastern Europe. To have published such a book at this time can hardly be taken as a very ecumenical gesture, even though the Uniat Exarch of Bulgaria, Mgr Courtief, told me it is a fairly objective piece of scholarship. These ten bishops and the Patriarch are clearly the majority in the Synod. It was they who decided that the Bulgarian Church should follow Moscow's lead and join the World Council of Churches four years ago, and it was they who decided not to follow Moscow and Constantinople in sending observers to the third session of Vatican II. Finally it was they who made sure that Bulgaria's stand on the question of dialogue with Rome at the Third Rhodes Conference should be one of extreme reserve.

There are three bishops who may be described as slightly more ecumenically minded than the above group, but they are still wary of Rome. In an interview with one of them, Mgr Kliment of Stara Zagora, I was told that the Orthodox had great hopes for the renovation of the Catholic Church through the work of the Vatican Council, but that he thought the third session had been conducted "under the cloud of *Ecclesiam suam*" which described the Orthodox as "beloved" but "separated" brethren. He said this encyclical had been a grave setback, since up till its publication the Orthodox had been under the impression that the dialogue was to take place on equal terms. Mgr Kliment said he thought *Ecclesiam suam* had been written under pressure from conservative cardinals. He was worried about discussion of the missions during the third session : "We are of course glad when the heathen are converted to Catholicism, but in Schema 13 proselytism is re-clothed in the word mission." The bishop stressed the impossibility of the

Orthodox entering into dialogue with Rome as long as proselytism continues. There has been none in Bulgaria since 1944, on his own admission, but he said that in recent contact with Greek bishops he learnt that the Uniats are still hard at it in Greece. The fact that the Greek Uniats suspended their proselytism twenty years ago is beside the point—the unfortunate thing is that the Bulgarian bishop firmly believes the inaccurate information put out by the Greeks to be true. In contrast to his wariness of Rome, Mgr Kliment was well disposed towards the other Churches. He felt that there are grounds for hoping that the Orthodox will achieve inter-communion with the Anglicans, Old Catholics and Monophysites in the relatively near future.

At the other end of the scale from the fanatical archimandrite monks are the ecumenically progressive Bulgars. These include the Oxford educated Bishop Nikodim of Sliven and a number of lay theologians who teach in the Theological Academy. Bishop Nikodim, who leads the Bulgarian delegation to the World Council of Churches, regrets the Bulgarian failure to send observers to Vatican II. He feels that the results of the Third Rhodes Conference were very much a necessary but disappointing compromise. Perhaps the most ecumenically minded Bulgar I met was one of the two young lay theologians who studied in Switzerland on World Council of Churches scholarships in 1963. Among other things he told me that it is hopeless to say, as many Orthodox do, that their religion contains the exclusive truth; it contains a large part of the truth, but there is much to be gained from contact with other Christians.

From an ecumenical point of view the above picture of the Bulgarian Orthodox Church may seem rather bleak, but there are at least three mitigating factors : (i) Most of the present bishops are ex-monks and the atmosphere in most Orthodox monasteries is hyper-conservative—in view of this it is surprising that more of the bishops are not fanatically opposed to contact with Rome; (ii) the wind of ecumenism has only been blowing on a few top members of the Bulgarian Church since 1961 when she joined the World Council of Churches; previously there had been little direct, personal contact with the West; (iii) only the Synodical bishops seem to be promptly and adequately informed of developments in Rome. Lay theologians I spoke to in the second week of December 1964 were still unaware of the decisions reached by Vatican II's third session that had ended a month before. Perhaps the greatest hope for the growth of an ecumenical climate among the Bulgarian Orthodox is that more young theologians may come to study in Western Europe under the auspices of the World Council of Churches.

appendix II
differences between catholicism and orthodoxy

ECCLESIOLOGICAL AND DOGMATIC DIFFERENCES

1. *Papal Authority*: while Catholic Church organization is based on the conception of Papal authority the Orthodox Church is exclusively ruled by synods, or councils of bishops. Supreme dogmatic authority is vested in the Ecumenical Synods (so far seven in number) while the local Churches are administered by local synods. The Orthodox would be willing to allow the Patriarch of Rome (the Pope) his ancient privilege of "first ranking", at the present time held by the Patriarch of Constantinople and otherwise known as the "primacy of honour".

2. *The Infallibility of the Pope:* while Catholics since 1870 have held that when the Pope pronounces *ex cathedra* on dogmatic matters his pronouncements are infallible, the Orthodox hold that the Holy Spirit only grants infallibility to the dogmatic decisions of a full ecumenical council. All the dogmas of the East date from the first seven Ecumenical Councils which took place prior to the Catholic–Orthodox schism.

3. *The Filioque clause:* in the Catholic conception of the Trinity the Holy Spirit proceeds from both the Father *and the Son*. The Orthodox hold that the Holy Spirit proceeds from the Father alone. While the feeling among both Catholic and Orthodox theologians is that the *Filioque* dispute is more of a mutual misunderstanding than a real theological bone of contention, on the popular level in Greece Catholic inclusion of this clause in the Creed is regarded as a serious error.

4. *The Immaculate Conception:* the Catholics believe in the Virgin's immaculate conception as a dogma. Some Orthodox have held Mary's conception to have been immaculate, while others have denied this. The latter say that the qualification of the Virgin as immaculate in the Orthodox liturgy refers to the purity of her life and not to her conception. The Orthodox object to the immaculate conception as a dogma since it has been unilaterally proclaimed by the West.

5. *The Assumption:* held as a dogma by the Catholics. Our Lady's assumption is accepted as a belief by the Orthodox, but they do not accept it as a dogma since it was proclaimed such by a Pope, and not by an ecumenical council.

6. *Purgatory:* the Catholics believe there is a state in the after-life in which a soul that will ultimately go to heaven is cleansed. The only two states in the after-life foreseen by the Orthodox are heaven and hell.

SACRAMENTAL AND LITURGICAL DIFFERENCES

(Some of these differences may seem minor to a Westerner brought up to differentiate sharply between symbol and meaning. To the Greek mind symbol and meaning are inextricably bound up—if the symbol is wrong the Greek person feels the meaning too must be warped.)

1. *The Bread of Consecration:* Catholics use unleavened bread for the consecration while the Orthodox use leavened bread.

2. *Communion:* from the Council of Trent until Vatican II Catholics communicated in one kind only. The Orthodox communicant takes both the bread and the wine. Catholic children make their first communion at about the age of seven; an Orthodox child can communicate any time after its baptism.

3. *Baptism and Confirmation:* the Catholics pour water over the person to be baptized. The Orthodox practise total immersion

and in Orthodoxy confirmation is administered immediately after baptism, while in Catholicism it is usually administered as a separate sacrament some time after the first communion.

4. *Celibacy*: all Catholic priests have to be celibate, with rare exceptions. Normally an Orthodox has to be married before he can be ordained, if he is to become a parish priest. Only monks and bishops have to be celibate.

5. *Divorce*: This institution is not admitted in the Catholic Church. The Orthodox Church allows divorce and up to two re-marriages. While the first marriage is regarded as a sacrament of joy and triumph, a second or third marriage has the character of a penitential sacrament.

(The items mentioned above do not constitute a total list of the differences between the two Churches; they are, however, the principal ones. The intention has been simply to list such differences without in any way going into their theological complexities.)

a select bibliography

(Greek texts are excluded from this list as being linguistically inaccessible to most English readers.)

SOCIOLOGICAL AND ECONOMIC:

Honour, Family and Patronage, J. K. Campbell (Clarendon Press, Oxford, 1964).

Vasiliká, E. Friedl.

Géographie Humaine de la Grèce, B. Kayser (Presses Universitaires de France, 1964).

Surplus Labour in Greek Agriculture, A. Pepelasis and P. A. Yotopoulos (Centre of Economic Research, Athens).

Greek Regional Development, B. Ward (Centre of Economic Research, Athens).

Farm Fragmentation in Greece, K. Thompson (Centre of Economic Research, Athens, 1963).

Six Villages d'Epire, H. Mendras (Unesco, 1961).

The Internal Migrant, C. Moustaka (Centre of Economic Research, Athens, 1964).

RELIGIOUS:

The Waters of Marah, P. Hammond (London, 1956).

L'Eglise Orthodoxe, O. Clément (Paris, 1961).

The Orthodox Church, T. Ware (Penguin, London, 1963).

Christian Greece and Rome, R. Etteldorf (St Paul's Publications, 1964).

The Orthodox Church, J. Meyendorff (Darton, Longman and Todd, London, 1965). (Translation from French text which appeared under the title *L'Eglise Orthodoxe hier et aujourd'hui*, du Seuil, 1960.)

The Church of Greece, E. D. Theodorou (Apostolikí Diaconía, Athens, 1959).

Orthodox Spirituality, by "a Monk of the Eastern Church" (London, 1945).

Orthodoxy—A Pan Orthodox Symposium (Zoi, Athens, 1964).

The Eastern Schism, S. Runciman (Oxford, 1955).

The Greek East and the Latin West, P. Sherrard (London, 1959).

Le Mont Athos, E. A. de Mendieta (Desclée de Brouwer, Paris, 1955).

Black Angels of Athos, M. Choukas (Stephen Daye Press, Brattlemore, Vermont, U.S., 1934).

Athos the Mountain of Silence, P. Sherrard (London, 1960).

Nostalgia for Orthodoxy, E. Mastroyiannopoulos (Zoi, Athens, 1959). (Translation from Greek.)

Repentance, S. Papacostas (Zoi, Athens, 1958). (Translation from Greek.)

Eusebius Matthopoulos, S. Papacostas (Zoi, Athens. (Translation from Greek.)

index